EVERYONE

PART 2
CHAPTERS 17–50

GENESIS

for

EVERYONE

PART 2
CHAPTERS 17–50

JOHN
GOLDINGAY

WESTMINSTER
JOHN KNOX PRESS
LOUISVILLE · KENTUCKY

© 2010 John Goldingay

First edition
Published by Westminster John Knox Press
Louisville, Kentucky

10 11 12 13 14 15 16 17 18 19—10 9 8 7 6 5 4 3 2 1

Quotations from Scripture are author's own translation.

Maps are © Karla Bohmbach and are used by permission.

Cover design by Eric Walljasper, Minneapolis, MN

Library of Congress Cataloging-in-Publication Data

Goldingay, John.
  Genesis for everyone / John Goldingay.
    p. cm. — (The Old Testament for everyone)
  ISBN 978-0-664-23375-4 (v. 2: alk. paper)
  ISBN 978-0-664-23374-7 (v. 1: alk. paper)
  1. Bible. O.T. Genesis—Commentaries.   I. Title.
  BS1235.53.G65   2010
  222'.11077—dc22
                                    2009028352

PRINTED IN THE UNITED STATES OF AMERICA

∞ The paper used in this publication meets the minimum requirements
of the American National Standard for Information Sciences—Permanence
of Paper for Printed Library Materials, ANSI Z39.48-1992

Westminster John Knox Press advocates the responsible use of our natural
resources. The text paper of this book is made from 30% postconsumer waste.

CONTENTS

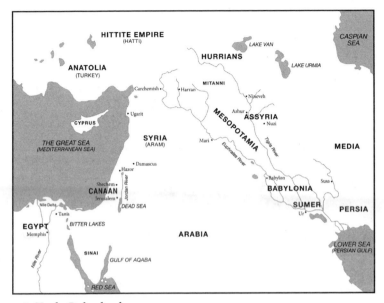

© *Karla Bohmbach*

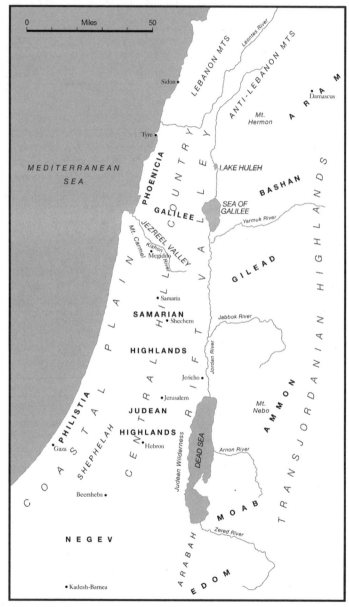

0   Miles   50

LEBANON MTS

Leontes River

ANTI-LEBANON MTS

A R A M

Sidon •

• Damascus

Mt. Hermon

Tyre •

PHOENICIA

COUNTRY

LAKE HULEH

MEDITERRANEAN SEA

BASHAN

GALILEE

SEA OF GALILEE

JEZREEL VALLEY

Yarmuk River

Mt. Carmel

Kishon River

• Megiddo

HILL

RIFT

GILEAD

VALLEY

TRANSJORDANIAN HIGHLANDS

• Samaria

SAMARIAN

Jabbok River

• Shechem

HIGHLANDS

Jordan River

COASTAL PLAIN

• Jericho

Jerusalem •

Mt. Nebo

AMMON

CENTRAL

JUDEAN

PHILISTIA

HIGHLANDS

DEAD SEA

• Gaza

SHEPHELAH

• Hebron

Judean Wilderness

Arnon River

Beersheba •

MOAB

N E G E V

Zered River

ARABAH

• Kadesh-Barnea

EDOM

© *Karla Bohmbach*

ACKNOWLEDGMENTS

The translation at the beginning of each chapter is my own. I have tried to stick closer to the Hebrew than modern translations often do when they are designed for reading in church, so you can see more precisely what the text says. Although I prefer to use gender-inclusive language, I have let the translation stay gendered if inclusivizing it would involve considerable paraphrasing of exactly what the text says.

At the end of the book is a glossary of some key terms that recur in the text (mostly geographical, historical, and theological terms). In each chapter (though not in the introduction), these terms are highlighted in **bold** the first time they occur.

I am grateful to Cheryl Lee for giving much of this book a nontheologian's read and telling me which bits didn't make sense. If they still don't make sense, it's my fault. I am also grateful to Tom Bennett for checking the proofs.

There are many stories in it about my friends as well as my family. None are made up, but where necessary to be fair to people, they are heavily disguised. Sometimes I have disguised them so well that when I came to read them again, it took me time to remember who it was they were describing.

GENESIS 17:1–6

Your Name Will Be Abraham

¹Abram was ninety-nine years old. Yahweh appeared to Abram and said to him, "I am El Shadday. Live your life before me and be a person of integrity, ²and I will make my covenant between me and you, and make you very, very numerous." ³Abram fell on his face; and God spoke with him: ⁴"Here is my own covenant with you. You will be the ancestor of a horde of nations, ⁵and you will no longer be called Abram. Your name will be Abraham, because I have made you the 'ancestor of a horde' of nations. ⁶I will make you very, very fruitful and make you into nations. From you kings will come."

Names are important. My middle name is Edgar, which was my father's first name. When I was being baptized, family legend says my grandmother leaned over to my mother and asked why it was not also to be my first name. My mother allegedly replied, "Because they will call his father Big Ed and him Little Ed" (which would be fine in the United States but would not work in Britain where "big head" suggests having too big an opinion of yourself). I don't think my parents realized that John is ultimately a shortened version of Johanan, "Yahweh showed grace," which is a neat name to be given. If they had realized, they would have been glad, because they had waited a while for the gift of a child. Names can suggest people's destinies or significance, or say something important about their parents' prayers for them.

So far, Genesis has been talking about "Abram." In Genesis 17 the name changes to the familiar form "Abraham." God brings about this change in connection with another reaffirmation of the promise to make Abraham into a numerous people, which God now expresses in a different way by declaring that Abraham will be the "ancestor" of a "horde" of nations. The first part of the name (*ab*) is the word for an ancestor or a father (in the New Testament, *abba* is the **Aramaic** equivalent). Now, if anyone wondered about the meaning of the earlier name Abram, they would probably conclude it meant "exalted father/ancestor." In a sense it already thus constitutes a promise of what Abram will be (there was nothing particularly exalted about him in his beginnings). And if you asked someone back in Harran what the name Abraham meant, they would probably say it meant the same as Abram (that is, these are two different spellings of the same name, like John and Jon or Ann and Anne). But in Hebrew, a "horde" is a *hamon*, so that within the name Abraham you can see most of that word (it is the business part of the name, too; *-on* is simply an ending, like the *-ing* on "ending"). On the basis of that, God can give a new significance to the longer, more familiar version of the name.

There are other significant aspects to what God says to Abraham. Genesis tells us that "Yahweh" appeared to Abram, but God's own self-introduction to Abraham is "I am El Shadday." **Yahweh** is the name God will reveal to Moses and the name by which God will be known to Israel. While Genesis knows that Yahweh is also acting and speaking in Abraham's day and is thus quite happy to use the name Yahweh, it also knows Abraham himself would not have used it. Names such as **El Shadday** correspond more to the way Abraham would have spoken. This usage signifies that the real God is involved here, the God who will be involved with Israel, but it preserves the distinctiveness of the way God would later speak to Moses.

God gives Abraham two significant biddings. First, he is to live his life before God. "Live your life" in Hebrew is the word literally meaning "walk," but it is a form of that verb that suggests walking about rather than simply making a single walk from A to B. It is the verb used of Noah's and Enoch's walking about or living their lives "with" God. Abraham is to walk his walk or live his life "before" God, which makes a different point. Abraham's walk will be one that God is watching and watching over, which is both an encouragement and a challenge. Both are significant in the context. God will be watching over Abraham protectively, as God has been doing through Abraham's ill-advised Egyptian adventure and his expedition to rescue Lot (Genesis 12–14), as he promised in Genesis 15 and will promise again here. God will also be watching to see what kind of person he is. Like Noah (Genesis 6:9), Abraham is to be a person of integrity. The word is usually translated "blameless," which makes it sound impossibly demanding.

But the word God uses suggests not the absence of any faults but the presence of a positive quality (which is, in a way, at least as demanding an expectation). More literally, God wants Abraham to be "whole," though in our context that would have psychological overtones. God wants Abraham to be wholly committed to God's ways. God doesn't expect him to be sinless; God is realistic and can cope with people making moral mistakes. Rather, God looks for a certain direction in people's lives, a certain cast to their lives, a fundamental moral wholeness or straightness.

In connection with that, God will make a **covenant** commitment to Abraham. Actually God has already done that, and Genesis 15 was clear that making the covenant did not issue from Abraham's being a person of integrity. He had not been that when they went down to Egypt. If Abraham made a contribution at all to the making of the covenant, it was simply by trusting in God's promise. Nor was the making of that covenant conditional on any acts Abraham would do. Yet God's commitment to Abraham was designed to involve Abraham's integrity, and if that integrity is not forthcoming, it is not clear that God's purpose in relating to Abraham can be fulfilled. Abraham's integrity was not the basis of the covenant, but it was essential to its working. In this sense, God can only go on affirming the covenant commitment if Abraham does the same. Otherwise (as with a marriage relationship) things will simply not work. It takes two to tango.

God repeats earlier promises about flourishing and about nations coming from him, and also adds the note about "kings."

GENESIS 17:7–8

Aliens and Strangers

> [7]"I will establish my covenant between me and you and your offspring after you throughout their generations, as an agelong covenant, to be God for you and for your offspring after you. [8]I will give to you, and to your offspring after you, the country in which you stay as aliens, all the country of Canaan, as an age-long holding, and I will be God for them."

There is a world of difference between being an alien and being a citizen. The *New York Times* has an ethical agony page where the columnist discusses some dilemma. Last week a reader was taking his family on vacation in Holland, where smoking pot is legal. Would it be okay to let his son do so there when it is illegal in the United States? he asked. Is it okay to smoke pot illegally in the United States if you think the ban on pot is a silly law? If I were looking at that question as an alien, a big consideration would be, "What would happen if I were found out?" A citizen risks a fine or imprisonment; I might risk deportation. I am in the United States only on sufferance. Taxation without representation is fine; as long as I behave, I am secure. But I do not have the security of a citizen. Aliens in the United States (or anywhere else) have even less security if they lack the right papers, and/or if citizens stop needing aliens to pick their lettuce or blow their leaves.

Genesis 12–16 has twice referred to the status Abraham and his people have as aliens in describing his position in Egypt and the position his descendants will eventually have in Egypt. In both contexts they will be aware of the insecurity attached to this status. It makes Abraham nervous about what will happen to Sarah (and to him!), and it will lead to his descendants being ill-treated by their hosts, as can happen to aliens in any country.

Solemnly, being an alien is also the position Abraham's family has in **Canaan** itself, and the position it will continue to have for generations. While things generally work out OK for them as aliens there, they have to live in areas that don't interest the Canaanites, and they have to go and find food elsewhere in a famine. So it is a significant promise that they will not always be aliens. One day the country will be their agelong or perpetual holding, and it cannot then simply be taken away from them. "Holding" most often refers to the tract of land that an individual family occupies; God allocates the country as a whole to the clans, and the clans allocate it to individual families, and no one can appropriate it. It is each family's secure possession. That is the position God promises that Israel will eventually have in relation to the whole country of Canaan. Genesis 15:16 has made clear it will be a long time before this can happen, because there is no basis at the moment for throwing the Canaanites out of the country. But when God can justifiably do so, it can become Israel's holding.

Given that eventually people in **Ephraim** and then many people in **Judah** will be **exiled** from the country, hearing about God's giving it to Abraham's descendants as an age-long or perpetual holding would raise questions and possibilities in the minds of listeners. The question would be how this loss of the country could have happened, though they should have little difficulty working that out; it is implicit in that comment about the Canaanites' losing the country because of their waywardness. If that can happen to the Canaanites, it can surely happen to the Israelites, as the **Torah** makes explicit. The possibility issues from that word "agelong" or "perpetual." English translations often use the word "everlasting," which may suggest too much. In the Old Testament, how long is agelong or how perpetual is perpetual depends on the context. The word can mean "through all your life." Maybe God simply means, "The country will be theirs as long as they live with integrity, but if they give themselves up to waywardness and fail to turn from that waywardness, they could totally lose it." But then, if in the context of exile people do turn back, this promise offers them hope. Maybe their exile is not the end. In the context of twenty-first-century politics, the implication would be that we can see the Jewish people's freedom to live unhindered in the country as an outworking of this promise that goes back to Abraham. But Genesis 15:16 would imply that God can hardly reckon that the Palestinian people can simply be thrown out of the country without reason in order to make that possible and that the Jewish people would be unwise to assume that God's real commitment to them excludes the possibility of their losing the country again.

The New Testament takes up the image of life as an alien to describe the position of Christians in the world. We are aliens there (1 Peter 1:1, 4, 17; 2:11–12). The idea is not that God's created world is not our home in the sense that we are just passing through it on the way to heaven. It is that we could not be citizens of the "world" because it works on a basis that has little to do with Christ. If we feel at home in *that* world, something worrying has happened to us.

5

Another basis for hope here is the link between the agelong or perpetual possession of the country and God's agelong or perpetual **covenant** with Abraham. God has described the covenant with Noah as a perpetual one; now that expression is used of this covenant. The expression again raises the question of the cash value of the word "agelong" or "perpetual." In making this commitment God might presuppose, "But of course all this assumes you stay faithful to me. If you do not do that, all bets are off." God will not terminate the covenant arbitrarily, but if Abraham's offspring withdraws, God will feel free to do so.

Christians have sometimes assumed that this is what God did when the Jewish people as a whole did not recognize Jesus, reckoning that the new covenant of which the New Testament speaks is made with the church rather than the Jewish people and that it replaces God's covenant with the Jewish people. In effect Romans 9–11 asks whether that might have happened. Paul's response is horror at the idea. How could the faithful God do that? It is as well God could not, he implies, because if God could terminate that commitment to the Jewish people because of its waywardness, then the church could be cast off in the same way. Actually God has not allowed the Jewish people to disappear, and they have been free to reestablish themselves in the country. This sign of God's faithfulness can make the church sleep easier in its bed.

In other words, God will continue to be God for Abraham and his offspring. God uses that expression three times.

GENESIS 17:9–14

A Sign of Grace, Commitment, and Discipline

⁹God said to Abraham, "And you, you are to guard my covenant, you and your offspring after you, through their generations. ¹⁰This is the covenant that you are to guard, between me and you and your offspring after you: the circumcising of every male you have. ¹¹You are to be circumcised in the flesh of your foreskin. It will be a covenant sign between me and you. ¹²As a child of eight days, every male among you is to be circumcised,

through your generations. The person born in the household and acquired for money from any foreigner, who does not belong to your offspring: [13]he is definitely to be circumcised, the one born in your household and the one acquired for money. My covenant in your flesh will be an agelong covenant. [14]But an uncircumcised male who is not circumcised in the flesh of his foreskin: that person will be cut from his kin. He has thwarted my covenant."

As was once the custom in Britain, my parents had me baptized when I was a baby, even though this was the only involvement they had with the church apart from weddings and funerals. I don't know exactly what they thought baptism was about, though I doubt if they regarded it as simply a social occasion. Given that they had waited a few years during which they had not been able to have a baby, they were thankful for my birth, and having me baptized would be a sign of this gratitude. When theologians seek to provide some further theological rationale for baptizing people as babies rather than waiting until they make their own profession of faith, they often emphasize that baptizing a baby reflects and testifies to baptism's being a sign of God's grace expressed in God's **covenant** with Israel that is then extended to the church. Yet baptism is indeed also a sign of someone's personal profession of faith, and baptizing people when they are in a position to make that profession matches that other aspect of its significance. Thus when I was a teenager and belonged for a while to a church that baptized people on the basis of their profession of faith, I was "rebaptized." (A bishop I know blows a fuse at that expression, because really you can be baptized only once and being "rebaptized" implies renouncing your first "baptism." So when someone who subsequently comes back to the Church of England wants to be ordained, he presses them to renounce their second "baptism." I don't think I have ever before come out with this shady event from my youth, so I may be in trouble.)

Both the baptism of babies and the baptism of people on profession of faith can thus have some theological rationale, and denominations that practice one or the other do not need to dismiss as misguided those that practice the other. In

Israel, whereas the later practice of bar mitzvah and bat mitzvah signifies a person's taking up a personal commitment to the **Torah**, the practice of circumcision testifies to God's grace. Male circumcision was a common custom among Middle Eastern peoples, as has been the case in many other societies, but it was generally applied to boys on the verge of adulthood, not at birth. Applying it when they are born reflects the fact that they do nothing to earn it. It was God who made the covenant with Abraham, which in this way comes to apply to them.

In another sense the rite of circumcision (like infant baptism) does indicate the need for response to God's grace. Paradoxically, this acceptance of responsibility is undertaken by the community as a whole, and in particular by the baby's family. They must guard or keep or protect God's covenant, and accepting the rite of circumcision is a way they do that.

While circumcision is the distinctive and exclusive sign of a distinctive and exclusive commitment to Abraham's family, God's instructions also emphasize that it does not apply to Abraham's birth family alone but to everyone in his household—to all those who are part of the family business, whether they have always belonged to it or whether they are like those further members of the household whom Abraham and Sarah acquired in Egypt or might have acquired as a result of the adventure in Genesis 14. While they are "only" servants, they belong so firmly to the family that the covenant also applies to them. It is another expression of the way God's involvement with Abraham and Sarah brings blessing through them to other people.

For us, some ethical questions are raised by the description of these people. It simply assumes it is okay for Abraham to have people in his household who count merely as long-standing "servants" (that word does not come here, but it is the status of many of the people "born in his household"). Indeed, it assumes it is OK for Abraham to buy people, but such people are not "slaves" in the sense of possessions you can do what you like with. Their being included in the covenant and thus given the covenant sign indicates that they are not treated as less than human. God's approach to their position is similar to the one the New Testament takes to actual slavery. God does not simply declare that the difference between masters and servants must be abandoned,

8

but God does transform the status of servants (home-born or bought) in their eyes and in the eyes of Abraham.

Receiving the sign will be the way to keep the covenant rather than breaking it, to guard the covenant rather than thwarting it. It is something important and valuable, so it needs guarding. The problem is not that someone else might steal it but that its "owners" might neglect it. It is fragile in the sense that disregarding it could imperil it, and declining to accept the sign of the covenant would indicate people were doing that. Those who do so do not imperil the existence of the covenant; but they do imperil their own share in it and risk being "cut" from their kin. You either accept one kind of cutting, or you experience another kind of cutting; you either get cut into the covenant that God has "cut" (Genesis 15:18), or you get cut out. God does not say that a person's kin are responsible for expelling a person who refuses the sign of the covenant, because Genesis is not laying down laws with sanctions. God's commands are more often the "Don't even think about it" kind of imperatives. To start thinking about penalties is to presuppose that people will disobey, which is unthinkable. On the other hand, while the covenant is radically inclusive, it is in another sense radically exclusive. Anyone can join, but those who decline to accept the covenant sign signify they want to stay outside the covenant family. If their kin accept the sign and thereby join, and they do not, they lose their place with their own kin as well as forgoing the chance to join this new kin. Only those who receive the sign are marked as within the covenant, but there is no ethnic or class bar to anyone receiving it. (We will consider its gender exclusivity in connection with 17:20–27.)

GENESIS 17:15–19

Sarai Becomes Sarah

[15]And God said to Abraham, "Sarai, your wife: she is not to be called Sarai, because her name is to be Sarah. [16]I will bless her and, yes, I am giving you a son from her. I will bless her and she will become nations; kings of peoples will come from her." [17]Abraham fell on his face, laughed, and said to himself, "Can a

child be born to a man of a hundred years, or can Sarah bear a child as a woman of ninety?" [18]So Abraham said to God, "If only Ishmael might live before you." [19]But God said, "Well, Sarah your wife: she is going to bear you a son, and you are to call him Isaac. I will establish my covenant for him as an age-long covenant for his offspring after him."

On my father's birth certificate, our family name is spelled Gouldingay. It was just a slip; I can imagine my grandfather and grandmother (hardly out of their teens) being a bit nervous when they registered the birth, and it seems they confused the registrar. But sometimes people change the spelling of their names more intentionally. I was myself once confused about spelling the name of a friend called Jonathan—or was it Johnathan? Some things that bore his name had the first spelling; others had the second. He eventually explained that he had originally used the first, more familiar spelling but had changed to the second in connection with other changes in his life. He knew he had to change the direction of his life and his lifestyle, and changing the spelling of his name was a symbol of that. Another friend adopted a quite new name when she entered a new stage of her life. There was nothing especially wrong about her old life; she just believed God was taking her into a new stage of life, and adopting a new name was a sign of that.

Sarai now becomes Sarah. For her, too, Genesis seems to see the point as lying in the mere fact of having a new name, not in something the name means. For people listening to these stories, "Sarai" would likely be simply a name; like most Western names, it would not have a particular meaning for them. It would be like Goldingay (which perhaps comes from the name of an English village where my ancestors lived, Golden Hay, a place with fine wheat fields; but people are not aware of that when they use my name). And in origin, "Sarah" may simply be a variant on "Sarai," like "Abraham" in relation to "Abram." But the listeners would know *sarah* as the word for a queen, princess, or lady and would see some significance in that name. Abram/Abraham had moved from having a name that would immediately mean something to people to one that would not in itself mean anything, though with imagination it could be understood

10

as making a point. Sarai/Sarah moves from having a name that would not mean anything to one that would mean something. The **covenant** turns Sarai into a queen, a princess, a lady.

While God does not point to this implication (it is the fact of the change that counts), the implication of Sarah's being a queen is hinted in what follows. She is to become the mother of nations, and kings are to be born from her, people such as Saul, David, Solomon, and the kings who will follow. In Britain we sometimes have a queen mother, usually the widow of a king who has died before her. Queen Elizabeth was the queen mother for over fifty years after the death of King George VI and the accession of her daughter, Queen Elizabeth II. A queen mother may not have institutional power, but she may have huge authority and significance for her people (when her husband was king and she was queen, Queen Elizabeth's spunkiness allegedly made Adolf Hitler call her "the most dangerous woman in Europe"). Sarah will be Israel's queen mother.

The mother of nations? Abraham falls down laughing. What kind of laugh was it? It is the first laugh in the Bible but only the first of a sequence of laughs we shall hear in this connection over the next few chapters; indeed, most of the laughs in the Old Testament come here. The combination of falling on the face and laughing suggests a significant pairing of reactions. Falling on the face is not the same as falling about. It is a posture of respect and submission, the posture a person takes to a king. Abraham had fallen on his face earlier in the chapter when God spoke about making a covenant. These are also the first times in the Bible when someone falls on his or her face before God, and the only times in the **Torah** when someone does so. Abraham's reaction hints at two forms of amazement, worshipful submission and a sense that God's promise is too good to be true, overtly expressed in Abraham's rhetorical questions to himself. These, too, are ambiguous in the impression they give of Abraham. Is his implicit answer "No" or "Yes"? God's answer to the questions will come when Sarah expresses herself in similar terms in Genesis 18: "Is anything too wondrous for Yahweh?"

As usual, we need not be too literal over the ages to which Abraham refers. Indeed, it may help us see the significance of the situation if we assume Abraham's and Sarah's actual ages were more like ones that would work with us. Can a woman of forty-five (especially one who has never been able to conceive) bear a child to an old man?

Perhaps Abraham does not know the answer to his questions. He does know that he and Sarah do not actually need a miracle in order for God to fulfill the promise to them and thereby to fulfill the promise about their being a blessing to the world. They have a son through Hagar. Won't he do as the means of bringing about this fulfillment? Could Ishmael not be the one who lives "before God"? The verb is different from the one God used to Abraham at the beginning of this chapter, but the "before you" will have similar implications. Could not Ishmael be the son God looks at, protects, and blesses? Ishmael is a teenager by now. Abraham has been loving him as his son for all these years. Perhaps he has been simply assuming that God's promises to him would be fulfilled through Ishmael; nothing in Genesis 17:1–14 would go against that. It is only when we come to God's words about Sarah that the bombshell drops for Abraham. Everything had seemed straightforward; suddenly he is again required to believe in the impossible. Couldn't God work through Ishmael?

God's answer contains both a yes and a no. God gives no reason for the no. In Genesis 18 we will find God operating in collaboration, dialogue, and negotiation with Abraham, but not in Genesis 17. You cannot second-guess God. Sometimes God says, yes; sometimes, no. Sometimes God gives reasons; sometimes God does not. It is worth asking, because you may get a yes, and it would be a shame to miss out because you are afraid of a no. It's like relating to a father or mother. On this occasion, God's mind is made up. The point is vividly expressed when God says Sarah "is going to bear you a son." More literally, God says she "is bearing you a son." God speaks as we do when we say, "I'm coming," when actually we are still finishing reading the newspaper. We mean that we are committed to coming and that we will definitely be there soon. And God indicates a commitment to Sarah's having this baby; he will definitely be there soon.

God does not point out that the name "Isaac" means "he laughs," exactly the verb form Genesis used just now when it said that Abraham "laughed," but presumably the people listening to this story smiled to themselves when they heard this. Isaac is the one through whom God's covenant promise will be fulfilled.

GENESIS 17:20–27

But What about Ishmael?

[20]"As for Ishmael: I have listened. Yes. I hereby bless him, and I will make him fruitful and make him very, very numerous. Twelve leaders he will father, and I will make him a great nation. [21]But my covenant I will establish with Isaac, whom Sarah will bear for you at this season next year." [22]When he had finished speaking with him, God went up from Abraham. [23]So Abraham took his son Ishmael and all the people born in the household and all those bought with his money, every male among the people in Abraham's household, and circumcised the flesh of their foreskin, on that very day, as God had spoken with him. [24]Abraham was ninety-nine years old at the circumcising of the flesh of his foreskin, [25]while his son Ishmael was thirteen years old at the circumcising of the flesh of his foreskin. [26]On that very day Abraham and his son Ishmael were circumcised, [27]and all the people in his household, those born in the household and those acquired with money from a foreigner, were circumcised with him.

When my sister and I were young children, our parents had a hard time making ends meet on my father's wages as a factory worker. My father was not keen on my mother going out to work while we were small, and eventually they decided to sell up and move to take over a mom-and-pop store in another part of the city where my mother could look after the store during the day while my father kept his factory job. It was the time when Britain was encouraging immigration from the Indian subcontinent and the Caribbean, and our part of the city became multicultural. We soon had people from Jamaica and Pakistan coming into the store looking for exotic foods such as rice (we knew rice only as something from which you made rice pudding for dessert). Although the people from Jamaica were Christian, they had a hard time fitting in because British churches were not very welcoming to them, but that is another story. The people from Pakistan raised quite different questions because they were Muslims. Eventually the city became the location of one of the first and largest purpose-built mosques in Western Europe, with a big sign outside that always makes me smile at its cleverness and chutzpah: "Read Al-Qur'an, the Last Testament." What were we as British Christians to make of people from the Indian subcontinent who transformed British cuisine but also transformed British religion? It was decades before I realized that the story of Ishmael provides part of the answer. Islam traces its history back to Abraham and Ishmael. It is respectful of the stories in Genesis, though it assumes that really Ishmael was the son who counted.

Genesis assumes Isaac is the son who counted, but at the same time it recognizes that God loves Ishmael. Promises of blessings and fruitfulness attach to him as they attach to Isaac. He, too, will become numerous. If we think only of the Arab peoples in the few hundred miles around Hebron and assume they can in some sense trace themselves back to Ishmael, that promise has certainly been fulfilled. Genesis 25 will already list twelve leaders descended from him.

So God's response to Abraham's prayer contains a yes as well as a no. "I have listened," God can say. God insists on fulfilling the main **covenant** promise through Isaac, but Ishmael can live before God, as Abraham asked, and Ishmael receives the covenant sign; he is embraced by the covenant. Perhaps Abraham did not relish the risk of hoping again for Sarah to conceive, a hope he may have felt free to give up once Ishmael was born. Yet he took on the risk of talking to God about it. He did not get all he asked, but he did get something. There are a number of prayers in the Bible like that. In this sense Abraham has indeed been involved in negotiation with God, the kind of negotiation and compromise that can happen between a person praying and the God who is prayed to, like the negotiation and compromise involved in relationships between parents and children. Abraham (or the child) has longings and hopes. God (or the parent) has a bigger picture of things that need to happen, a bigger canvas to fill out. God (or the parent) may find the concrete request hard to fit into the bigger canvas; the suppliant (or the child) may not get all he or she wants but may get something that is much better than nothing.

The story closes with Abraham's implementing the commission about circumcision, which will have been a monumental undertaking (the darkly comic aspect to the story in Genesis 34 will illustrate the point), but Genesis quite ignores all that. Its interest lies in the quality of Abraham's obedience to God. "On that very day," it twice notes. "All" and "every" male was involved, it notes four times. Twice it itemizes the way this commitment embraces people born within the household and people brought into it from outside. One reason the Old Testament likes repetition is to draw attention to the total nature of the way people do what God says. Abraham makes sure there are no mistakes and no exceptions. He knows total commitment is necessary, and he sees total obedience happens.

The account of the implementation unconsciously emphasizes another aspect of the chapter that may seem troublesome. There is no ethnic or class bar in respect of the covenant sign, but there is a gender bar. It is odd that God instituted a covenant sign applying only to males. It is not as if only males count as members of the covenant or as if females have to approach God through the male members of their family. Women are as free and obliged as men to pray, worship, bring sacrifices, and obey the **Torah**. Perhaps it is significant that with circumcision, as with practices such as sacrifice, God is not devising something new but adapting something from the culture. And we may feel rather glad that God did not institute female circumcision alongside male circumcision (there is said to be some evidence for female circumcision in Egypt, but none for elsewhere in the Middle Eastern world in ancient times).

In other words, it might seem odd that God instituted as a covenant sign this particular rite rather than others one could imagine. In Israel, Nazirites grew their hair as a sign of their dedication to God. A sign of that kind would have been possible. God commissions Israelites to bind commands from the Torah onto their hands and foreheads (Deuteronomy 6:8), which orthodox Jews at least take as literal and not just metaphorical injunctions; a sign of that kind would have been possible. A servant who wants to commit himself to his master for life has his ear pierced (Exodus 21:2–6). Ear piercing or an earring would have been a possible sign. Why a mark on the male sexual organ? It is the organ that gets men into trouble, and the organ that got Abraham into trouble in his own way in begetting Ishmael. It complicates things when a man's sexual activity is not subordinated to God. Although it also complicates things when a woman's sexuality is not subordinated to God, in most cultures men have felt and had more freedom to ignore that principle. The Old Testament will go on to talk about the need for ears to be circumcised, and for hearts or minds to be circumcised, but it begins with the need for sexuality to be circumcised. Men's sexuality is to be cut down to size.

GENESIS 18:1–15

Entertaining Angels Unawares

[1]Yahweh appeared to him by the terebinths of Mamre, when he was sitting at the entrance of the tent as the day grew hot. [2]He looked up and saw, and there, three men were standing opposite him. When he saw them, he ran to meet them from the door of the tent, bowed to the ground, [3]and said, "My lords, if I have found favor in your eyes, do not pass by your servant, please. [4]May someone get a little water? Bathe your feet. Rest under the tree. [5]I must get a bite of food. Refresh yourselves, then you can pass on, since you have passed near your servant." They said, "Yes, do as you said." [6]Abraham hurried to the tent to Sarah and said, "Hurry, three measures of fine flour, knead it, make bread." [7]Abraham ran to the herd, got a nice, tender calf, and gave it to a boy, who hurried to prepare it. [8]He got curds and milk and the calf that he had prepared and set it before them, and stood opposite them under the tree as they ate.
[9]They said to him, "Where is your wife Sarah?" He said, "There, in the tent." [10]He said, "I will definitely come back to you next year. Yes: there will be a son for your wife Sarah." Sarah was listening at the entrance to the tent, which was behind him. ([11]Abraham and Sarah were old, advanced in years; Sarah had stopped menstruating in the way woman do.) [12]So Sarah laughed to herself: "After I am withered is there going to be enjoyment for me, with my lord old?" [13]But Yahweh said to Abraham, "Why did Sarah laugh, saying 'Am I really going to give birth, when I

am old?' ¹⁴Is something too wondrous for Yahweh? At this season I will come back to you next year and there will be a son for Sarah." ¹⁵Sarah lied, saying, "I did not laugh," because she was afraid. But he said, "No, you laughed."

One of my friends thinks she may once have met an angel. She was driving to work along a stretch of road surrounded by open land in a well-to-do part of the Los Angeles area, and she passed someone who looked rather like a homeless man, walking his bicycle. It was not a place where she regularly saw bicycles, and it was not clear what the man would be doing there and why he would be walking. She felt compelled to turn back and (against her usual principle) to give him some money. When he looked at her through the driver's window "his eyes were radiant—glowing, almost," she said. "As I drove on to work I said to myself, 'That was an angel.' And I felt a bit shaken up."

It is a plausible notion. It overlaps with (or turns upside down) the premise of a long-running TV series, *Touched by an Angel*. When we arrived in the United States, I was astounded to find such a program on network television, and also astounded to discover that it got angels right. The word *angels* tends to suggest female figures with wings, in flowing white dresses. The angels or **aides** in the Bible are not like that. They are humanlike; you may not realize you have met one, at least at first (hence the comment in Hebrews 13 about entertaining angels unawares). The angels in *Touched by an Angel* looked human, except (if I remember rightly) that a glow appeared around them when they revealed themselves to be more than just the human beings they have so far seemed to be as they have been seeking to help someone with a crisis in their life. In a similar way, director Wim Wenders portrays two angels who look after Berlin in his film *Wings of Desire* as middle-aged men in shabby raincoats. (One of them starts to glow—at least, the movie goes Technicolor—when he realizes his desire to become a human being.)

Genesis 18 begins by telling us that *God* appeared to Abraham, but this is the headline to the story, and it will be some time before Abraham realizes the identity of his mysterious visitors. When three humanlike figures show up at his encampment, there is nothing to suggest that they are anything other than three men. It is often said that Abraham offers them typical desert hospitality, though his hospitality looks more extravagant than anything anyone would regularly offer. If they were three men who needed just a burger to keep them going for the next leg of their journey, their eyes would surely roll when they realized Abraham was setting about killing the fatted calf. And one dare not think what the assertive but ninety-year-old Sarah mutters when Abraham rushes in with the message "I need you to bake three loaves, and I need them *now*." It is said that when the prodigal father *runs* out to meet the prodigal son, he is behaving with a lack of dignity that would be unaccustomed for a respectable Middle Eastern man, and the same would apply to Abraham. In other words, the entire story underlines the extravagant nature of Abraham's hospitality.

The question "Where is Sarah?" relates to the fact that the message that follows is directed to her as much as to Abraham. Perhaps it is in keeping with the norms of the culture that strange men and the woman of the household stay somewhat distanced from each other (and maybe that stopped people from getting into some of the messes we get into with our more relaxed attitude to relationships between the sexes). But the spokesman for the three visitors wants to make sure she hears what he says. He speaks *to* Abraham, but he speaks *about* Sarah as much as about Abraham. That had been so in Genesis 17, but there was no mention of Sarah's being party to what God said; here, God makes sure that she is. Keeping her ears pricked, just inside the tent, will do.

What she hears makes her laugh, as Abraham had laughed on that occasion in Genesis 17. But Sarah's laugh is less ambiguous. What the man says is just impossible. She knows her own body. (It is not clear whether she is commenting on the unlikelihood of her having sexual pleasure or the unlikelihood of her experiencing the joy of motherhood.) In response to that, God speaks. As we might have guessed in light of the story's headline, the spokesman is the one among the three who is or who represents God. But again this is something the audience gets to know because the storyteller makes it explicit; neither Abraham nor Sarah know, though maybe the explicit reference to God points to the likelihood of their starting to realize that these are not just three ordinary passersby. On the other hand, the person who the storyteller has told us is God refers to God in the third person ("Is something too wondrous for Yahweh?"). This suggests that at most it would be only a growing realization.

Sarah's skepticism is understandable. It would take a miracle to bring about what this man says. Somehow, Sarah has to break out of her framework of expectations for what is possible. Let's suppose she would accept that nothing is too wondrous for God to bring about. She would also know that God is economic with miracles. They would not be called wonders if they happened every day. I can perhaps accept that they happen extraordinarily to other people, but when someone starts suggesting I am about to experience one, accepting that is a different matter.

God has no sympathy with this logic, but neither does God say, "Well, if you don't believe, it won't happen." Human faith is neither here nor there. What counts is God's intention. The existence of Ishmael makes no difference to God's intention to do something wondrous through Sarah, and the disbelief of Sarah makes no difference either. This puts us in our place and rescues us from the burden and guilt of thinking that everything depends on us.

Somehow Sarah has indeed worked out that there is something more to these three visitors, or at least to the spokesman, and she is afraid. You do not have to be afraid just because three ordinary crazies show up at your tent with implausible messages from God. Her fear tells us she knows she has gotten into something scary. Illogically, she tries to talk her way out of the situation, but she cannot do so. Even that does not put God off from giving her the gift of a child, because it's not about her. It's about God's purpose.

GENESIS 18:16–20

The Cry from Sodom

[16]From there the men got up and looked down at Sodom, with Abraham going with them to send them off. [17]But Yahweh said, "Am I going to hide from Abraham what I am doing, [18]when

Abraham is indeed to become a great and powerful nation, and all the nations on the earth are to bless themselves by him? [19]Because I have recognized him so that he may charge his children and his household after him to guard Yahweh's way by showing faithfulness in the exercise of authority, so that Yahweh may bring about for Abraham what he has spoken concerning him." [20]So Yahweh said, "The outcry of Sodom and Gomorrah, it is great. Their offense, it is very grave."

Any day I write, there are cries arising from the world. To test that statement, I just went to get today's newspaper. On the front page is a photo of a woman who lost a leg and whose husband and son died in a NATO bombing in Afghanistan. In the inside pages are further photos and accounts of people who lost limbs and/or family members. Other news items report the fighting between government and Tamil rebels in Sri Lanka and between opposing forces in Darfur. Their cry arises to people who read newspapers or watch television reports or documentaries, and we (at least I) find it hard to watch or read them properly partly because it can seem we can do nothing about the horrendous human suffering they bring to our attention. Earlier today I went to seminary chapel and heard one of my colleagues describing her involvement in supporting and counseling aid workers in such contexts. The cry gets to them, and they have to know what to do with it and how to live with it.

A similar cry goes up from Sodom and from Gomorrah. As far as we know, it does not reach Abraham, but it reaches God. It transpires that this cry is the reason the three "men" are on their way past Abraham's camp. As they begin to resume their journey, God again speaks, only this time the speaking is happening inside God. Usually when we would refer to "thinking" something, the Old Testament talks about "saying" it; sometimes it adds "in his heart," but sometimes it just says "said," as here. It's a piece of inner reflection.

God has some intentions with regard to one of the peoples Abraham knows about and has interacted with. In this connection God picks up the promise to Abraham from back in Genesis 12. Abraham is destined to be a means of blessing coming to the nations; you could say he has already been that for Sodom and Gomorrah and the other cities in Genesis 14. He has a key place in God's purpose for the world. As God put it, "I have recognized him." Translations usually have "I have called him," which is fair enough as a paraphrase, but the actual word God uses is the ordinary word for "know" or "acknowledge." It is the word that comes when God says, "I recognized" Jeremiah in his mother's womb (Jeremiah 1:5), or says to Israel "You are the only people I 'recognized'" (Amos 3:2). It implies singling out and making a commitment to someone. In light of that "recognition," Abraham needs to know what God is planning for this bit of the world to which Abraham is supposed to be a blessing.

By deciding that Abraham should be aware of that, God is treating him as someone like a prophet such as Jeremiah. The Old Testament knows that God does not sit alone in heaven deciding on policies and implementing them. God has a cabinet of the people we call angels, divine **aides** who join in the process of decision making and decision implementing. The aide who went to sort things out with Hagar (Genesis 16) was an example, and the aides who accompany Yahweh in this story are also examples. But many people listening to this story know how someone like Isaiah or Jeremiah is also made an honorary member of God's cabinet. Such prophets can listen into its debates, volunteer to act as its agents (or try to get out of it), and protest at its decisions and urge it to do something else.

In effect, Abraham is being admitted to their company. Or in this particular story, it's a little like the seminary president going to see someone on the staff who wasn't in the cabinet and saying, "I had better tell you a decision the cabinet made this morning." It would give that person the chance to say, "Did they make allowance for X?" That is what Abraham will do in a moment.

By implication, the fulfillment of God's purpose in recognizing Abraham (that is, his being a blessing to the world) requires that he manage his household properly. His household is of course much bigger than what we would think of as a household or family; Genesis 14 has already indicated that there are hundreds of people in it. So he needs to make sure that authority is exercised and decisions get taken there in a faithful and right way. God uses for the first time another pair of words that would remind Genesis's audience of the prophets. The prophets are always going on about what translations call "justice and righteousness." The trouble is that they use a pair of words for which we do not have equivalents in English.

For us, "justice" suggests fairness, treating everyone the same, while "righteousness" suggests living a proper, upright personal life. Whatever the importance of fairness and uprightness, they are not the ideas conveyed by the words translated "justice and righteousness." The first word means something like the authority to make decisions. These decisions are of course to be made in a just way, but there can be such a thing as "unjust justice," decisions taken in an unfair way, and this shows that the word does not in itself mean "justice." The second word occurred once before in Genesis 15:6, when Abraham made his act of trust in God "and he counted it for him as faithfulness." It counted as doing the right thing by the other person in the context of a mutual relationship. So a key motif in Abraham's family's life (and thus in Israel's life, the prophets emphasize) is that decisions should be taken and authority exercised in a way that honors other members of the community and their mutual commitment. It means doing the right thing, doing the faithful thing. That is the way Abraham will "guard Yahweh's way." Those principles of action are the heart of God's own way of acting in the world, and that is a key reason that they need to characterize the way Abraham's people act in the world. Here, too, God is saying something whose significance Abraham will take up in a moment.

The problem is that life in Sodom and Gomorrah is not like that at all, and God has heard the outcry about it. There is a neat and horrible link between the Hebrew word for doing right by people and the word for an outcry. The two words are the same except for one letter. As Isaiah 5 puts it, God looks for *sedaqah* (people doing right by one another and God, being faithful to one another and God) but what God sees is *se'aqah* (people crying out because of the way other people treat them). "Outcry" also recalls how Genesis 4 described Abel's blood "crying out." It anticipates how the Israelites will cry out when they are oppressed in Egypt (and on many subsequent occasions), and how God will listen to their cry and take action in relation to it.

God listens to the cry of people in Sodom and in Egypt. Does God listen to the cry of people in Afghanistan and Sri Lanka and Sudan? Accounts of God's listening to people's cry invite us to join in the cry of such people and make the kind of loud noise God will be unable to ignore.

GENESIS 18:21–33

On Praying for Sodom

[21]"I must go down and see whether they have acted totally in keeping with the outcry that has come to me. If not, I must recognize it." [22]The men turned from there and went to Sodom, while Abraham was still standing before Yahweh. [23]Abraham drew near and said, "Are you really going to sweep away the faithful with the faithless? [24]Perhaps there are fifty faithful people within the city. Are you going to sweep the place away and not carry it for the sake of the fifty faithful people within it? [25]Far be it from you to do a thing like this, killing the faithful with the faithless, so that the faithful and the faithless are the same. Far be it from you. Is not the one who exercises authority over all the earth to exercise authority?" [26]Yahweh said, "If I find fifty faithful people within the city, I will carry the whole place on account of them." [27]Abraham replied: "Well: I have undertaken to speak with my Lord when I am dirt and ash. [28]Perhaps the fifty faithful will be five short. Will you destroy the whole city for five?" He said, "I will not destroy it if I find there forty-five." [29]He spoke yet again to him: "Perhaps forty will be found there." He said, "I will not act, on account of the forty." [30]He said, "May fury not come over my Lord, and I will speak. Perhaps thirty will be found there." He said, "I will not act if I find there thirty. [31]He said, "Well, I have undertaken to speak with my Lord. Perhaps twenty will be found there." He said, "I will not destroy it on account of the twenty." [32]He said, "May fury not come over my Lord, and I will speak one last time. Perhaps ten will be found there." He said, "I will not destroy it on account of the ten." [33]Yahweh went when he had finished speaking to Abraham and Abraham went back to his place.

Yesterday we prayed in church, as we usually do, for God to grant peace and goodwill among nations. It is tempting to feel cynical about such prayers. Does God listen to them? Do they make a difference? Would it make a difference if we gave up praying for the nations (many churches do not do it)? But I remember someone suggesting that churches praying for peace and justice in the world may do more to hold back the forces of disorder than all our diplomatic activity to this end. At least Christians need to be wary lest being active in politics and social action alongside agnostics and atheists makes us forget also to do the vital thing that agnostics and atheists won't do, to pray for the world. Abraham's conversation with God supports that comment. Thinking about it over the years has made me add praying for the nation to my own prayers, where I confess it did not have a place before.

Abraham is drawn into praying for Sodom. God has heard the cry from the city, and the object of the expedition into which Abraham has been drawn is to check out whether the cry has exaggerated its picture of what is happening down there. Excuse me, but does God not know for sure what is happening just through being God? Does God really need to come and look? But Genesis recurrently describes God asking questions and checking things out. You may interpret such statements metaphorically if you wish, but you would have to ask yourself why you are doing that and to be careful of what you are missing out on. The description of God coming down to look makes the point that God does not stay up there in the heavens apart from what is happening in the world, insulated by omniscience and unaffected by events. It can seem that politicians in Washington or Westminster are in danger of making decisions without having any experience of the real lives of the peoples for whom they are making decisions. God does not risk that danger. God comes to look. God sees people's suffering and sees the people who bring it about. In Jerusalem, the king lives on the height of the city, able to look down over it. It is his vocation to do that, to look over the palace walls at what is happening in the city and act on what he sees. God operates like that.

And if things are actually not as they have been reported, God must "recognize" it. God neatly reuses the verb that was featured in connection with Abraham. God needs to know people and situations and to make decisions on the basis of that knowledge; and God does so. God's looking means God makes sure decisions are made on a proper basis.

This question dominates the subsequent conversation between Abraham and God. It is not exactly a prayer insofar as Abraham never asks God to do anything. One of its significances is to discuss one of the trickiest of theological questions, nowadays described as the question of theodicy. Is God really just? How do you reconcile the idea of God's justice with the unfairness of much that we see in the world? When NATO bombs Afghanistan, it does not just affect the bad guys; "innocent people" suffer, too. When God summons the king of Babylon to destroy Jerusalem in 587 BC, it affects faithful people such as Jeremiah as well as people who worshiped other gods. That's not fair. But life is like that; the innocent do suffer with the wicked.

Sometimes the Bible simply shrugs its shoulders at that fact, but here it declines to do so, at least in this context where God is taking the initiative (this is not merely human beings acting unfairly to other human beings). It does not exactly solve the problem. It rather establishes that it is a problem for God, too. We might think that God does not have to make tricky decisions, that for God everything is black and white, but this story makes explicit a point underlying the whole biblical story. For decade after decade in Israel's story, God has to make tricky decisions about whether people's conduct has become so bad that action can no longer be postponed. Such decisions involve a judgment call. Abraham's questioning brings that out. God sometimes does bring judgment on a city even though there are fifty faithful people there. But God recognizes that questions can be raised about whether this is right. Like us, sometimes God has to choose between courses of action, neither of which is very good.

Here is where it is so significant that the conversation between Abraham and God is a kind of prayer. It means a person such as Abraham can always question the judgment call and ask whether it should go the other way. God has to weigh the relative importance of corporate justice and individual fairness. God has decided on this occasion to give priority to the first principle. But God also accepts the second principle, so Abraham can argue on its basis.

What Abraham first urges is that God should "carry" Sodom in its waywardness. Translations use the word "forgive"; it is the word most commonly translated "forgive" in the Old Testament. But it is the ordinary verb for "carry," and it provides a vivid image of what we do when we forgive people. Instead of making them carry their wrongdoing and its consequences and burden, we do so. Paradoxically and boldly, Abraham suggests that this is the way God must exercise authority in the world, by carrying the people who reject that authority and will not live God's way. Abraham cunningly turns back on God's description of him as a person who is to act faithfully and rightly in exercising authority and turns to guard God's own way. In effect Abraham says, "You know you were talking about the faithful exercise of authority and its being the way I have to safeguard? Well, I have a question to raise about that. . . ." In prayer we urge God to be God, perhaps differently from the way God is currently planning to be God. We do it with due deference; Abraham several times refers to the fact that God is his Lord (remember that when English translations have the word *Lord*, usually *Lord* replaces God's actual name, but here it is that word *Lord*). We are just God's servants, but we do it.

The close of the story encourages us further in this connection. We might have thought Abraham was here speaking with God. But the story closes by referring to God's having been speaking with Abraham. That fits the way the account of the prayer starts with God's hanging around after the departure of the other two "men," almost as if to ask, "Is there anything you want to say to me before I go, Abraham?" Abraham is indeed like a member of the heavenly cabinet whom God wants to involve in the process of decision making about what happens on earth. His prayer takes place within God's purpose, not against it.

GENESIS 19:1–14

The Sin of Sodom

¹The two aides came to Sodom in the evening, and Lot was sitting at the gate of Sodom. Lot saw them, and got up to meet them and bowed, his face to the ground. He said, "Now, my

lords, please do turn aside to your servant's house so you can spend the night and bathe your feet and go on your way early." They said, "No, we can spend the night in the square." ³But he pressed them strongly, so they turned aside to him and came to his house. He made a banquet for them and baked flat bread, and they ate. ⁴Before they could go to bed, the men of the city, the men of Sodom, surrounded the house, young and old, the entire people, from every part of it. ⁵They called to Lot and said to him, "Where are the men who came to you this evening? Bring them out so that we can have sex with them." ⁶Lot went out to them at the entrance but shut the door behind him. ⁷He said, "Please, my brothers, do not do this wrong. ⁸Now, please: I have two daughters who have not had sex with a man. Let me bring them out to you and you can do to them whatever you like. But do not do anything to these men, because they have come under the shelter of my roof." ⁹But they said, "Get over there," and said, "The man came to stay as a guest and he is actually exercising authority. Now we will do worse to you than to them." They pressed hard against the man, against Lot, and moved forward to break the door. ¹⁰But the men stretched out their hands and pulled Lot to them, into the house, and shut the door. ¹¹As for the men who were at the entrance to the house, they struck them with a daze, young and old, so that they became weary of trying to find the entrance. ¹²The men said to Lot, "Who else do you have here, sons-in-law, sons, daughters, anyone who belongs to you in the city? Take them out of the place. ¹³Because we are going to destroy this place, because the outcry before Yahweh against them has become so great that Yahweh has sent us to destroy it." ¹⁴So Lot went out and spoke with his sons-in-law, who were to marry his daughters, and said, "Up, get out of this place, because Yahweh is going to destroy the city." But in the eyes of his sons-in-law he seemed like someone who was trying to make them laugh.

I have a number of friends and acquaintances who are attracted to members of the same sex or are in long-term, committed, quasi-marital or actually marital relationships with members of the same sex. I don't take the view that same-sex relationships are just as valid as heterosexual relationships, but neither do I think they are inherently more terrible than various other ways of falling short of God's vision for sexual relationships. But one thing that strikes me is that my gay friends and acquaintances are lovely people. A few years ago, for instance, our neighbor was diagnosed as having Parkinson's disease, and because my wife is disabled, his partner would talk with me about the issues involved in long-term care for the person you love. Eventually he came to the realization that he needed to reshape his life and get a less demanding job and think about early retirement in order to be able to care for his partner, and in order to do so they left our condo complex where they were very much at home and part of the community. There are nasty gay people as there are nasty straight people, but straight people can demonize gay people.

It has been commonly assumed that the clear condemnation of the homosexual act that the men in Sodom wanted to commit indicates the stance the Scriptures take in relation to contemporary same-sex relations, but the story does not concern a form of same-sex relationship that anyone seeks to defend as proper or morally acceptable. Further, God is taking action against Sodom because of the "outcry" that has made itself heard in heaven, and when the Old Testament talks about an outcry, it is referring to the violent way weak people are being treated by powerful people. The implication is that the issue in Sodom is the affliction of the powerless by the powerful. If God cannot find even ten faithful people there, maybe that indicates that the cry is one uttered by the blood of people who have been slain in the city, a cry like that of Abel's blood. Or maybe the cry relates to Sodom's oppressive relationship with the countryside around; the city is often a parasite on the countryside. The total faithlessness and violence of the city is indeed illustrated by the desire of the entire community to see Lot's visitors raped.

In its entirety the story is horrible, and over the chapter as a whole it is not going to improve. It reminds one of some midnight movie that no normal respectable person goes to see. As is often the case, the Bible shatters our understanding of what a Bible should be. But this is partly because the story recalls not only late-night movies but also stories we hear about things that actually happen. It acknowledges that Sodom is the real world—where God is involved, angels are involved, and the people of God are involved. The Bible is not escapist literature.

There is some irony about the story. Lot is sitting in the gate area at the entrance to the city, a natural place to watch the world go by, and his welcome of the two **aides** (again without knowing who they are) closely resembles the way Abraham had acted. It is the arrival of the men from the city that makes the story somersault into a nightmare. Lot's hospitality thus contrasts starkly with theirs. They have no desire to welcome strangers. Their desire to rape the men illustrates how rape commonly has nothing to do with sexual desire but everything to do with power and humiliation. Yet what does Lot think he is doing in offering them his daughters? Perhaps he knew the men would not accept them; having sex with them would not meet their desire to subjugate the two visitors. But at best, that is a high-risk policy.

The outcome of the scene is to establish the point God and the two aides had come to establish. No wonder the outcry against Sodom had reached God's ears. Perhaps the implication is that the two aides were by no means the first to receive the kind of welcome the city wishes to give them, and others would not have the supernatural powers of defense that these two had. The scene provides compelling evidence for the truth of the aides' exhortation to Lot that he needs to get out of here. Yet this is not how it seems to his sons-in-law. (In our terms they are apparently his potential sons-in-law; they do not seem to be in Lot's household, but if they were engaged to his daughters they might be seen as already having an in-law relationship with him.)

There is another irony in their assuming that Lot was only joking (as Genesis more literally puts it), because they use the verb "laugh" that has a prominent place in these stories. Sarah thought God was only joking in promising her a son; these young men think Lot is only joking in warning of disaster. Furthermore, there is only one letter's difference between the Hebrew words for "cry out" and "laugh." The sons-in-law have not heard the outcry from Sodom, so they can laugh at the idea that God would be destroying it. If everyone in the city surrounded Lot's house with their horrifying plan must they not have been among them?

GENESIS 19:15–38

Don't Look Back

¹⁵As dawn came, the aides pressed Lot, saying "Up, take your wife and your two daughters who are here, so that you are not swept away because of the waywardness of the city," ¹⁶but he delayed. So the men seized him, his wife, and his two daughters by the hand, by Yahweh's mercy on him, and brought him out and put him down outside the city. ¹⁷When they had brought them outside, one said, "Flee for your life, don't gaze behind you, don't stop anywhere in the plain. Flee to the mountains, so that you are not swept away." ¹⁸But Lot said to them, "Oh no, my Lord! ¹⁹Now. Your servant has found favor in your eyes. You have showed such great commitment to me in preserving my life. But I—I cannot flee to the mountains so that the disaster will not overtake me and I die. ²⁰Here—this city is near for flee-ing to, and it's small. I can flee there—it's small, so that my life can be preserved." ²¹He said to him, "Okay, I am granting your request with regard to this matter, as well, in not overthrowing the city you spoke of. ²²Hurry and flee there, because I cannot do anything until you arrive there." Hence the city was called Smalltown. ²³As the sun rose on the earth and Lot arrived at Smalltown, ²⁴Yahweh rained on Sodom and Gomorrah burning sulfur from Yahweh, from the heavens. ²⁵He overthrew these cities and the entire plain and all the inhabitants of the cities and what grew in the ground. ²⁶But Lot's wife gazed behind him and became a salt column.

²⁷Abraham went early in the morning to the place where he had stood before Yahweh ²⁸and looked out over Sodom and Gomorrah and all the region of the plain. He looked and there, smoke from the region rose up like the smoke from a furnace. ²⁹So it was that when God destroyed the cities of the plain, God was mindful of Abraham and removed Lot from the midst of the overthrow, when he overthrew the cities in which Lot lived.

³⁰Lot went up from Smalltown and lived in the mountains, his two daughters with him, because he was afraid to live in Smalltown. He and his two daughters lived in a cave. ³¹The firstborn said to the younger, "Our father is old and there is no one in the world to sleep with us in the way of all the world. ³²Come on, let's get our father to drink wine so we can sleep with him and preserve offspring through our father." ³³So they

got their father to drink wine that night and the firstborn went in and slept with her father. He did not know when she lay down or when she got up. ³⁴Next day the firstborn said to the younger, "Now. I slept with my father last night. Let's get him to drink wine tonight as well, and you go and sleep with him, so we can preserve offspring through our father." ³⁵So they got their father to drink wine that night as well, and the younger one got up and slept with him. He did not know when she lay down or when she got up. ³⁶Thus Lot's two daughters became pregnant through their father. ³⁷The firstborn bore a son and called him Moab. He is the ancestor of Moab to this day. ³⁸The younger also bore a son, and called him Ben-ammi. He is the ancestor of the Ammonites to this day.

The English make jokes about the Irish and use the word *Irish* as a term of opprobrium; it is a way of saying something is stupid. Other ethnic groups behave in similar ways; Portuguese people and Brazilians make jokes about each other. The Irish also make jokes about the English, sometimes turning their own alleged stupidity into canniness, thus inverting the logic of the humor, and it is also the case that the Irish make jokes about the Irish. But I am English, so my responsibility is to reflect on why we make jokes about the Irish. There is a general answer; everybody needs some other group to make fun of. And a specific answer lies in the history of England and Ireland: that is, it reflects the quasi-colonial position that Ireland has often occupied in relation to England and the related role of Irish immigration in England. Nowadays I stop myself using the word *Irish* as a term of opprobrium.

Israelites listening to this story likely sniggered in a similar way. Among other things, it could seem to offer an explanation of the origins of two of Israel's neighbors, an explanation that made fun of them. The name "Moab" is similar to an expression that would mean "from my father." Ben-ammi, "son of my people/kin," is similar to the word for an Ammonite, *ben-Ammon*. I do not know of any anti-Ammonite jokes in the Old Testament, but there is an anti-Moabite joke in Isaiah 25 that seems to describe Moab as swimming in "dung" on the basis of a similarity between that word and the name of a Moabite city. Once again, the Bible is not a respectable, middle-class, bourgeois, Western book. It enables us to see how culturally relative are some Western attitudes.

Indeed, maybe the story came into being to provide pretend answers to questions people asked. Why is the Dead Sea region so inhospitable? Why is there such a smell of sulfur? Why are there those columns made of salt (in Hebrew the Dead Sea is the "Salt Sea")? Where did the Moabites and the Ammonites come from? Voilà: here is an explanation for all that. I say "pretend answers," because I then assume Genesis 19 is one of the chapters where we are further away from anything you would ever have read in the *Jericho Times*. Yet it is not "just a story"; we can see aspects of it that might have made God OK about having it in his book.

One recurrent motif is the need to be prepared to take action when God is about to act. Lot seems to be a figure who is torn. In the New Testament, 2 Peter 2 emphasizes his recognizing how perverted Sodom has become. But the story shows he has also been pulled down by it, to judge from the offer of his daughters (and does the last episode in the story show how they have also been affected, or been affected by their father's being affected?). He has to be dragged out of Sodom, literally and metaphorically. And he wants to stay as near there as possible. It seems that Lot doesn't get it. The phrase "run for the hills" in the traditional English translations is not an exhortation he wants to heed.

There is the need not to look back. The verb suggests more than a mere casual glance. Lot's wife is also torn. Perhaps she is imagining the potential sons-in-law they have had to abandon. Her gaze is another expression of hesitation, an awareness of what she will lose by allowing God to pull her out of a city like Sodom, and she becomes frozen in her gaze. Psalm 139 talks about the need to hate people who are opposed to God and God's ways. As when Jesus talks about hating one's parents, it's not talking so much about hatred as a feeling but about hatred as a total disavowal of people who will lead us in the wrong way. "Remember Lot's wife," Jesus bids his disciples (Luke 17:32).

There is the fact that in all this, God is mindful of Abraham's prayer. It was "by God's mercy" that the **aides** did not respond to Lot's delaying tactics by saying, "Suit yourself; we're

outta here." It was because Lot "found grace," not because he
deserved anything, and because the aides had shown **commitment** to him; Lot sure knows how to use the right theological
words even when he is trying to avoid doing what God's agents
say. By implication, Abraham had been trying to persuade God
not to destroy Sodom, but he had not mentioned the idea of
rescuing Lot's family from there. Yet apparently this happened
because of Abraham's prayer, which made a difference to what
God did, even though it was a different difference from the one
Abraham had in mind.

And there is the reminder of the desperate lengths to which
people can be driven by tumultuous events in life. As usual,
Genesis does not pass explicit judgment on the two daughters.
As far as they can see, their action is the logical result of the
position they have been put in, though their conviction that
Sodom's destruction means there are no men left in the world
implies an odd ignorance about their Uncle Abraham's family. But their parents have taken their daughters to a grim fate
that reflects the way they have all been shaped by living near
Sodom. What else are the girls to do?

GENESIS 20:1–13

Do We Ever Learn?

¹Abraham traveled from there to the region of the Negev and
lived between Kadesh and Shur. When he stayed in Gerar,
²Abraham said of Sarah his wife, "She's my sister." So Abimelech
the king of Gerar sent and took Sarah. ³But God came to
Abimelech in a dream by night and said to him, "Now. You are
a dead man because of the woman whom you have taken. She
is a married woman." ⁴Now Abimelech had not approached her.
He said, "Lord, would you slay a nation even if it is faithful?
⁵Didn't that man say to me, 'She's my sister,' and she also said,
'He's my brother'? It was with integrity of attitude and with
innocence of hands that I did this." ⁶God said to him in the
dream, "Yes, I know that you did this with integrity of attitude,
and I myself have indeed kept you from offending against me.
Hence I did not let you touch her. ⁷So now give the man's wife
back. Because he is a prophet, he can intercede for you. Save

your life. But if you do not give her back, recognize that you will definitely die, you and everything that is yours."

⁸Early in the morning Abimelech summoned all his servants and repeated all these things in their hearing. The men were very scared. ⁹Abimelech summoned Abraham and said to him, "What have you done to us? How did I offend you that you have brought a great offense upon me and upon all my kingdom? You have done deeds with us that should not be done." ¹⁰And Abimelech said to Abraham, "What did you see that you did this thing?" ¹¹Abraham said, "I said, 'There is definitely no reverence for God in this place, and they will slay me for the sake of my wife.' ¹²And also, she really is my sister, my father's daughter, admittedly not my mother's daughter. So she became my wife, ¹³and when God made me wander from my father's household, I said to her, 'This is the commitment you must show to me: Every place we come to, say about me: He's my brother.'"

There was a man who used to come to talk to me from time to time when he had gotten into a mess with a woman (well, he came at other times, too). He was married and ought to have known better, but he didn't. He would blame the women: they were attractive, or they were needy, or they threw themselves at him. He would blame his wife: she was no longer interested in him; she was only interested in her work; she was no longer interested in sex. He had a hard time blaming himself, though eventually he managed to do so. Putting it that way reflects how this could have been a move from one immature attitude to another immature attitude. But eventually he did make the transition from merely blaming himself to accepting responsibility for his actions in a more constructive way. What brought about something of a breakthrough was the fact that the last time he got into a mess it was a really big one. But as a result he came to acknowledge more deeply where his weaknesses lay and to see where he needed to be wary about the way he related to women. If he was right that some of those women, at least, did throw themselves at him, I don't know that he is invulnerable if it happens again. But he has more insight and more prospect of doing the right thing.

I don't know if Abraham ever reached that point, but the ploy he tries in Gerar he has already tried in Egypt (Genesis

12), and here he ends up telling us that his action there and here were only two instances of his implementing his regular policy as he moved about! He has long been expecting Sarah to show her **commitment** to him in this way! His son will make the same mistake (Genesis 26), suggesting how consistent we married men are at getting into a mess in relation to the opposite sex. His attempt to defend himself to Abimelech gets him into more trouble than he was in already (as defending yourself often does), at least in our eyes.

Another irony in the story is its more explicit emphasis (compared with the story in Genesis 12) on the foreign king's integrity. Abraham is convinced there is no reverence for God here and no respect for other human beings (he thinks Abimelech would kill him to get Sarah). It turns out Abraham is projecting. It is Abraham who has no reverence for God and no respect for other human beings. Christians sometimes fret at the way non-Christians can behave with more integrity than Christians, and we are right to do that, but at least we can be comforted by the way there has always been this dynamic about relationships between the people of God and other people.

Abimelech knows that having sex with Sarah when she is another man's wife would be a terrible thing to do and that even doing so in innocence does not mitigate the act a great deal. The conviction that adultery is "the great offense" appears in the writings of other Middle Eastern peoples, though as far as I know they do not make explicit why they see it this way. It is a big temptation. Married men do indeed get into a mess about sex, and when they do so, it has a distinctive capacity to destroy community relationships as well as to devastate a family. (Murder is no doubt a worse sin, but it is probably a lesser temptation.) God confirms Abimelech's estimate of its seriousness. Perhaps God exaggerates in implying adultery would lead to death; God does not demand the death penalty of adulterers such as David. But speaking in these terms makes clear that God, too, sees it as "the great offense" or at least "a great offense." In Abraham and Sarah's case it also imperils the fulfillment of God's intention to bless the world through their family, which will be why God gets involved in a dramatic way in this particular situation. Abraham's being prepared to risk the fulfillment of God's purpose doesn't mean God is prepared to do so.

We are then rather astonished to find God encouraging the relatively godly Abimelech to get the relatively ungodly Abraham to pray for him, and doing so on the basis of Abraham's being a prophet. While this was in effect the position Abraham occupied in praying for Sodom in Genesis 18, it is the first time the word "prophet" is used in this connection—or any connection. A prophet is someone admitted to God's cabinet and free to speak there, and it is this freedom that God invites Abimelech to get Abraham to use. Abraham's membership of the cabinet was not based on his being a godly person; it is just based on God's choice of him for that position. So his ungodliness does not mean he cannot fulfill the role God chose him for, because that depends on God's sovereignty and God's choice, not on something about him that made him deserve to be given this role.

GENESIS 20:14–21:14

At Last

¹⁴Abimelech took sheep and oxen and male and female servants and gave them to Abraham, and restored his wife Sarah to him, ¹⁵and Abimelech said, "Now. My country is before you; live where you please." ¹⁶To Sarah he said, "Now. I am giving your brother a thousand pieces of silver. Now: it will be cover for everyone who is with you and with regard to everything, and you are vindicated." ¹⁷And Abraham interceded with God and God healed Abimelech and his wife and his maidservants, and they had children (¹⁸because Yahweh had totally closed every womb belonging to Abimelech's household because of Sarah, Abraham's wife).

²¹:¹Yahweh indeed dealt with Sarah as he said. When Yahweh did for Sarah as he had spoken, ²Sarah became pregnant and bore Abraham a son in his old age, at the season of which God had spoken. ³Abraham called his son, who had been born to him, whom Sarah had born to him, Isaac. ⁴Abraham circumcised his son Isaac when he was eight days old, as God charged him, ⁵Abraham being a hundred years old when his son Isaac

was born to him. [6]Sarah said, "God has made laughter for me, since everyone who hears will laugh in connection with me," [7]and she said, "Who would have announced to Abraham, 'Sarah has nursed children'? But I have born a son in his old age."

[8]The child grew and was weaned, and Abraham made a great feast on the day that Isaac was weaned. [9]But Sarah saw the son of Hagar the Egyptian, whom she bore Abraham, laughing. [10]She said to Abraham, "Throw out this maidservant and her son, because this maidservant's son is not to inherit with my son, with Isaac." [11]The matter was very distressing to Abraham because of his son. [12]But God said to Abraham, "Do not be distressed about the boy or about your maidservant. Whatever Sarah says to you, listen to her voice, because it is through Isaac that offspring will be named for you. [13]The son of the maidservant: I will make him into a nation, too, because he is your offspring." [14]Early next morning Abraham took food and a skin of water and gave them to Hagar. He put them on her shoulder, and the child, and sent her away. She went, and wandered about in the Beersheba wilderness.

My parents married later in life than was usual in their day, and I previously mentioned that it was some years before I was born. My mother used to tell me she couldn't imagine there was a baby more welcomed into the world than I was. A generation later when my wife and I married, we thought we could decide when to start a family but found we did not decide; a week after it was confirmed that Ann was unexpectedly pregnant, the *British Medical Journal* carried an article reporting that the contraceptive pill she was taking was less effective than some others, a fact that we were able to confirm. The unexpected baby was still very welcome. Another generation later, people often choose to delay marrying and then delay having a baby for career reasons, and then decide it's time. . . . And sometimes this works out fine, but sometimes they, too, discover they have less control over these matters than they thought.

I imagine there could be some competition for designation as the world's most welcome baby, and that Isaac would be in the running for it. But before we come to this story, there are some other wombs that need opening. Another implication of the story of Abraham and Abimelech is the scary way our actions can risk consequences for other people's lives. That is obviously so for Sarah when Abraham lets her be taken into the king's harem (again!), though Genesis does not comment on that. Despite her agreeing to collaborate, one can imagine the feisty Sarah we know from Genesis 16 having a thing or two to say about this if we could ask her. But Abraham's action also brings consequences for the king and people of Gerar, on whom the story focuses. Toward the end of the story we discover that God prevented any of the women in the royal household from conceiving, not as a permanent disability but as a temporary loss that would force the king to look at what was going on.

As was the case in Genesis 12, the irony here is that all the nations of the world are due to bless themselves by Abraham, and we have been reminded in Genesis 18 not only of this fact but also of Abraham's vocation to teach his family to do the right thing by one another and thus guard God's way. All this unravels before our eyes. Abraham fails to do the right thing by Sarah and by the family they do not yet have, and he brings trouble rather than blessing on Abimelech and his household. One can imagine God rolling his eyes and realizing, "I am going to have to sort all this out again."

So God appears to Abimelech. There is another neat reversal here. Abraham was supposed to be a means of blessing but is a means of trouble. Abraham is elsewhere the one to whom God appears, but God can appear to a foreign king, both for the king's sake and for the sake of God's purpose. There is that final irony that even though Abraham is so in the wrong, he still has a place in God's cabinet, so he can still plead Abimelech's case and get an answer.

The women in Abimelech's household are thus able to conceive again. Even more astonishingly, Sarah also does so. And great would be the rejoicing at Isaac's birth. There is the birthing, the suckling, the naming, the circumcising, the growing, the weaning, and the feasting. Oh yes, this is a boy whose name speaks of laughter, whose mother laughs, and whose birth will bring a smile to countless people who hear of it.

But his birth cannot be the uncomplicated event it was designed to be. Indeed, in the way the story is told, it is soon overshadowed by subsequent events. Isaac is the person whose name stands for laughter, a laughter in which Sarah rejoices. But there is someone else laughing in the story, and Sarah cannot handle that. When she sees Ishmael "laughing," to her it is as if he is pretending to be Isaac, as if he is trying to take Isaac's place. So she acts to rule that out.

And God agrees that there is a problem or a danger here. Ishmael was not part of God's plan, and God did not want to change the plan as a result of Sarah and Abraham's taking the action they did in getting Hagar to have a baby on Sarah's behalf. Why did God not want that? Genesis does not say. Why did God not close Hagar's womb? That would have simplified things. Genesis does not say. Yet once Sarah, Abraham, Hagar, and God have worked together to bring Ishmael into the world, he cannot simply be ignored. Sarah wishes he could; Abraham cannot get away from the fact that Ishmael is his son. Sarah may not want to accept any responsibility for him and for Hagar, but God will do so. In Genesis 16 God has already made an undertaking with regard to Ishmael; Genesis 21 is a rerun of Genesis 16, as Genesis 20 was a rerun of Genesis 12 (once more, do we ever learn?).

GENESIS 21:15–32

On Watching Your Son Die

[15]When the water in the skin was finished, she left the child under one of the bushes [16]and went and sat herself down at a distance, a bowshot away, because (she said), "I am not going to watch the child die." So she sat down at a distance and wept aloud. [17]God listened to the boy's voice, and an aide of God called to Hagar from the heavens and said to her, "What is happening to you, Hagar? Don't be afraid, because God has listened to the voice of the boy where he is. [18]Get up, lift up the boy, take him by your hand, because I am going to make him into a great nation." [19]And God opened her eyes and she saw a well of water. She went and filled the skin with water, and got the boy to drink. [20]God was with the boy. He grew and lived in the wilderness, and became a bowman. [21]He lived in the Paran wilderness. His mother got a wife for him from the country of Egypt.

39

²²At that time Abimelech and Phicol, his army commander, said to Abraham, "God is with you in everything that you do. ²³So now, swear to me here by God that you will not deal falsely with me or with my offspring or with my posterity; you will act towards me and towards the country in which you are staying in accordance with the commitment that I have shown towards you." ²⁴Abraham said, "I do swear." ²⁵But Abraham complained to Abimelech concerning a well of water that Abimelech's servants had seized. ²⁶Abimelech said, "I do not know who did this thing. You have not told me; I have not heard of it until today." ²⁷Abraham took sheep and oxen and gave them to Abimelech, and the two of them sealed a covenant. ²⁸Abraham set apart seven ewes from the flock. ²⁹Abimelech said to Abraham, "What are these seven ewes here that you have set apart?" ³⁰He said, "You are to accept the seven ewes from my hand so that it will be a witness that I dug this well." ³¹Hence that place was called Beer-sheba, because the two of them swore an oath there. ³²When they had sealed a covenant at Beersheba, Abimelech and Phicol, his army commander, set off and went back to the country of the Philistines.

Today I read about the death of the young son of the leader of the opposition party in the U.K. parliament. The boy had been born with cerebral palsy and a severe form of epilepsy, and in a sense his parents had been watching him die all through his six years. They sometimes slept on hospital floors to be with him in a crisis. For them, he was the most beautiful and the most precious child in the world. But they had to watch him die. His father's chief political adversary, the prime minister, who had himself once lost a child, commented that "the death of a child is an unbearable sorrow that no parent should ever have to endure."

Even if God or Abraham told Hagar about the renewed undertaking God had made, one can imagine it doesn't count for much when you have wandered in the wilderness for long enough to have run out of water, when you know your child is dehydrated, and when you know that this is how people die in the wilderness. But God intervenes, as God did not for that little boy with cerebral palsy.

God does so because of listening to Ishmael's cry, not because of seeing Hagar's tears, but I guess either way would be fine with Hagar. She knows that God is one who sees and also one who listens; that is what Ishmael's name means, Genesis 16 notes. God here lives up to the boy's name. If you have had to watch a child die, I guess you will have mixed feelings about this boy's story. In one sense, stories about God's raising people from the dead, healing people, or rescuing people from oppression are little use to most of us because God does not do that for us; they may seem more hurtful than comforting. Yet they may also be an encouragement. They declare that our experience is not the only reality, and they open up possibilities for hope and bases for prayer; God has been known to rescue people in this way, so maybe God might do that for me. . . .

Was the well there all the time, but had Hagar not seen it? Sometimes there are resources available to us that we do not spot, but we must be wary of blaming Hagar for not seeing resources that were present. The story does not make her responsible for the tragedy that would have unfolded if God had not intervened. It rejoices in the fact that God did intervene.

So the story of Hagar and Ishmael gets its fresh start. God is with Ishmael. He is the first person about whom that is said; it will recur as a promise for Isaac (Genesis 26:24), but it is first said of the boy who does not count in terms of the great purpose that God is set on accomplishing. You do not have to be Isaac (or Jewish) to have God with you, turning you into a great nation. You can be Ishmael (or Arab).

After the pathos of the story of Hagar and Ishmael, the story of Abraham and Abimelech is very down-to-earth. Abraham continues to be settled in the south of the country. To talk about the country as a whole, you might use the expression "from Dan to Beersheba": Dan is on the far northern border (it is still the border between Israel and Lebanon and Syria), and Beersheba is the southernmost town before the land becomes desert. The southwest of the country is where the Philistines later lived, in and around the region we call the Gaza Strip; they were not there in Abraham's day, but for later readers of Genesis it makes sense to refer to this as "the country of the Philistines." Ancient Beersheba is a particularly spectacular archaeological site, and one of its most stunning features is a well outside the city's main gate. You can stand there and imagine the scene in this chapter

unfolding (unfortunately, there is no indication that this particular well existed in Abraham's day, but you can still use your
imagination . . .). "Beer" is the word for a well, and "sheba" is the
word for "seven," while it is also similar to the word for swearing
an oath; Genesis works with both these facts.

While the story explains how Beersheba got its name, it does
more than that. It begins with quite a confession by Abimelech:
"God is with you in everything you do." Abimelech continues
to be a foreigner of some insight. In Genesis 20 he could com-
plain (in effect) that Abraham was supposed to be a means of
blessing but became a bringer of trouble. Here he gives a con-
trary testimony. Genesis has just told us that God was "with"
Ishmael. Although it has never said that about anyone else, one
could reckon it applied to various people. Now Abimelech says
it about Abraham. He can see it in the way things work out for
Abraham. It implies God has fulfilled the promise to be Abraham's God. Abimelech is wise enough to want to be associated
with that rather than trying to work against it. So another aspect
of God's promise is being fulfilled. Abimelech wants to have a
positive relationship with the people where God is at work.

In negotiating that relationship, Abimelech uses two key
Old Testament words, **commitment** and **covenant**. He uses
them not in a theological or religious context but in a political
one, which reflects how the Old Testament assumes that the
political and the religious interweave. Personal and political
relationships provide us with ways of thinking about relationships between God and us; the way relationships between God
and us work out ought to have a spin-off in the way political
and personal relationships work.

Connected to this is the straightness of the way Abraham
and Abimelech deal with one another. The Abraham stories
come in pairs: there are two stories about God's making a
covenant with Abraham, two stories about Hagar, and so on.
This is the second story about Abraham's dealing with conflict.
When there was tension between his staff and Lot's staff, he
did something about it (Genesis 13). Now there is tension with
Abimelech's staff, and he does something about it. Abraham is
prepared to take decisive and aggressive action when someone
else has been improperly treated (Genesis 14). When his own

interests are involved, he is decisive and talks straight but does so in order to be a peacemaker.

GENESIS 21:33–22:2

The Test

> [33]He planted a tamarisk at Beersheba and called there in the name of Yahweh, God Forever. [34]Abraham stayed in the country of the Philistines for a long time.
> [22:1]Some time after this, God tested Abraham. He said to him, "Abraham!" And he said, "I'm here." [2]He said, "Take your son, your only one, the one you love, Isaac, and get yourself to the region of Moriah, and offer him as a burnt offering there, on one of the mountains that I will tell you about."

I am writing at the beginning of Lent, and I have been thinking about the story of Jesus' forty days in the wilderness, when he was led by the Spirit into the wilderness to be tempted by the Devil. Every time I get to the end of that sentence, I have to go back to the beginning and wonder how its two halves can fit together. Jesus was led by the Spirit into the wilderness, yes. Jesus was tempted by the Devil, yes. But Jesus was led into the wilderness *to be tempted*? Apparently so. One of the clues to understanding what was going on is that whereas English has different words for "testing" and "temptation," the Old and New Testaments use the same words for a positive testing designed to build you up and a negative temptation designed to pull you down. The King James translation in fact has God here "tempting" Abraham. Jesus' temptation was also a testing from which he could emerge the stronger to begin his ministry. Adam and Eve's temptation was also a testing, which they failed. Abraham's testing was also a temptation, which he resisted. Every testing is a temptation; every temptation, a testing. When the man of whom I spoke in connection with Genesis 20:1–13 is tempted to get involved with another woman, it is also a test. If and when he resists that temptation, he has also passed a test and emerged from the experience a bigger man, a more mature man.

Abraham's testing follows on his reaching a new insight regarding who God is. He has resolved his relationship with

Abimelech and watched him disappear towards the horizon, leaving Abraham in a secure position in the Beersheba area. As well as breathing a sigh of relief, he turns to God to express his recognition that it was God who makes this possible. On other such occasions he has built an **altar**, but on this occasion he plants a tree. We do not know why there would be that difference, but it corresponds to the importance of trees elsewhere in his story, apparently as places where it would be natural to worship. The first place where God appeared to him was the oak at Moreh (Genesis 12). Now there is a tamarisk, a bushy tree more at home in the dry climate of the Beersheba area.

For Melchizedek in Genesis 14, God is **El** Elyon, "God Most High," and Abraham was prepared to speak in similar terms of God, though he saw the need to make explicit that this God was also "**Yahweh**." In Genesis 16 Hagar became a theologian and recognized that Yahweh was also El Roi, "The God Who Looks for Me." In Genesis 17, Yahweh appeared to Abraham as **El Shadday**. Here Abraham calls Yahweh also El Olam. Like most of those other names, this one is hard to provide with a succinct English equivalent. "Olam" means something like "the age" or "ages," as when we say that something has lasted "for ages" or will last "for ages." For Abraham to call Yahweh El Olam is to say that as far back as could be imagined Yahweh has been God and has been involved with him and that Yahweh will be God and will be with him as far into the future as could be imagined. He is God Forever, which can imply forever backwards as well as forever forwards. This is the only occurrence of this title in the Old Testament, though it sums up an assumption that runs all through. God has said that both the **covenant** with Noah and the covenant with Abraham will last "forever" or be "agelong" and that God will give Abraham the country "forever" as an "agelong" possession. Abraham now attaches that word to God's own person, no doubt with the conviction that the significance of this for him is that God will always be God for him.

You might think the story of Abraham and Sarah is working toward its end, and in a way it is. They have their son. They have a secure position in the country. The country does not exactly belong to them (whatever that would mean), but no one is disputing their right to be there. A long time passes. Yes, Yahweh has been proven to be "God Forever" for them. Whatever we make of their actual ages, they have reached old age. Yes, their story is surely working toward its end. Then there is a bombshell. Some time later, God decides on this test for Abraham.

With hindsight, we can see that the chapter forms an appropriate climax to Abraham's story as a whole. It again forms a pair with an earlier story. God's bidding, "Get yourself" to Moriah to a place that I will tell you, pairs with God's original bidding in Genesis 12, "Get yourself" from your father's household to a country that I will show you. These are the only two places in the Old Testament where this expression comes. It is almost as if the Abraham story could not come to an end without God saying once again, "Get yourself. . . ." But a crucial difference this time is not only that the story starts within the country where God had sent Abraham but that it presupposes God's having dealt with one of the big issues in the background to that first story. There God was promising to turn Abraham into the ancestor of a great nation, notwithstanding Sarah's infertility. Now Sarah has the son whose existence opens up the way to God's fulfilling this promise. Yet God's second "Get yourself" imperils that promise.

God's words underline the heartrending nature of the bidding. "Abraham!" "Yes?" "You know your son?" "Yes." "He is your only son, isn't he?" "Yes." We might find this an odd exchange, since Abraham has two sons. As far as God is concerned, perhaps he is the one son who counts in terms of the fulfillment of God's purpose. Further, whereas in light of Sarah's not having conceived, Abraham had said to God, "If only Ishmael might live before you," perhaps Isaac is now the one son who counts for Abraham too. But another consideration lies behind the designation. Sarah is Abraham's only "primary wife." Hagar is also Abraham's wife, and in Genesis 25 we will read of a third wife, Keturah, but it is explicit there that Keturah is a "secondary wife," and it is also implied that this was also Hagar's status. Being a primary or secondary wife need not imply anything about the love or commitment your husband has for you; it likely relates mainly to your children's inheritance rights. In this legal connection Isaac is indeed Abraham's "only" son.

45

So God says, "You know your son, your only son?" "Yes, Isaac." (In case there is any doubt here; and he is the son who brought such joyous laughter). "Yes," Abraham says. "You love him don't you?" (It is the first reference to love in the Bible.) "Oh, yes," says Abraham. "Kill him for me, then, will you?"

"God tested Abraham." We might be inclined to turn the story upside down and reckon that sacrificing his son was not a test from God but a temptation Abraham ought to resist. A Jewish tradition raising an inverted form of this question appears in the Talmud, a collection of traditions put into writing during the centuries following New Testament times. Such stories handle the questions that a thoughtful person listening to the biblical stories might raise. Surely God could not issue such a command? In the Talmud's elaboration, Satan appears to Abraham when they are on their journey to Moriah and tempts him to sacrifice a lamb instead of his son. Abraham has to resist that temptation. In another version, Satan points out to Abraham how implausible it is that God should give Abraham a son in his old age and then expect Abraham to sacrifice him. It just does not make sense. And he points out how immoral the act will be. But Abraham knows that he has to resist such logic when he has heard God speak.

Within Genesis, the focus lies specifically on the fact that Isaac is not merely any son but the son through whom God will keep the promise to Abraham to fulfill a purpose for the world. The stories of Abraham and Sarah have described a number of ways in which God's promise has been imperiled, by circumstances (such as Sarah's infertility) or human failure (such as Abraham's penchant for giving Sarah away). Now God personally imperils that promise.

GENESIS 22:3–10

On Letting Your Son Die

³So early next morning Abraham saddled his donkey and took two of his boys with him, and his son Isaac. He cut the wood for the burnt offering, set out, and went to the place that God told him about. ⁴On the third day, Abraham looked up and saw the

place from a distance. [5]Abraham said to his boys, "You stay here with the donkey. The boy and I will go over there and worship, and come back to you." [6]Abraham took the wood for the burnt offering and put it on his son Isaac, and took in his own hand the fire and knife, and the two of them walked together. [7]Isaac said to his father Abraham, "Father!" He said, "I'm here, my son." He said, "Here are the fire and the wood, but where is the sheep for the burnt offering?" [8]Abraham said, "God will see to the sheep for his burnt offering, my son." So the two of them walked together. [9]They came to the place that God had told him. There Abraham built the altar and laid out the wood and bound his son Isaac and put him on the altar on top of the wood. [10]Abraham reached out his hand and took the knife to slay his son.

What on earth does it do to you to have your father go to the edge of killing you? What does it do to your relationship to your father, and what does it do to your view of God? A seminary colleague of mine in England, who (like me) was also a Church of England priest and served a little at a local parish church, on one occasion reenacted the story of Abraham's offering of Isaac in a family service. Our two families lived in adjacent houses on the seminary campus. Our children were of similar ages and were always in and out of each other's houses (through the walls I remember listening to the boy involved in this reenactment doing his piano practice early on a Saturday morning when I thought I had the right to an extra hour of sleep). Watching the reenactment was horrifying. It brought home the horrific nature of the event (though it doesn't seem to have done the boy any harm; he grew up to be a fine, balanced adult).

It is significant that God bids Abraham to sacrifice his son and also that in the end God does not want him to do so. God wants to test Abraham's obedience and trust, and Abraham passes the test. Bidden by God to set about this task, he gets up early next morning to start the journey. Genesis likely presupposes that everyone would be aware of Moriah's location; 2 Chronicles 3 identifies Mount Moriah as the place where the temple was built. Either Abraham must know the place, or the story includes the name at this point because that is the place God will in due course point out to him. Nor do we know why he told his "boys" to stay behind while he and Isaac went to worship. Is it that they will try to stop him, or that this event is between God and Abraham?

There is a contrast between Abraham's reaction to this bidding by God and his reaction when he knows what God intends to do to Sodom. The earlier bidding led him into prayer, into asking whether God really means it. This bidding does not have that effect. Why might that be? One difference between the two stories is that the first relates to Abraham's concern for someone else while the second relates to Abraham's concern for himself. We might think it relates to Isaac, but the story focuses on Abraham rather than Isaac. It is about testing Abraham, about Abraham's willingness to do what God says even when it is outrageous, when it concerns the fulfillment of God's own purpose, and when it goes against Abraham's feelings as a father. We might again compare it with Jesus' statement that it is impossible to be his disciple unless we hate father and mother, wife and children, brothers and sisters, and even life itself (Luke 14:26).

The story is about God and Abraham. It brings to our attention the way we might see our relationship with God as entirely a matter of—well, us and our relationship with God. Prayer is then about my getting God to do what I want for me. Genesis 18 suggests that our relationship with God and our prayer is not so much about us and what we need as about other people and what they need. Genesis 22 now suggests it is not so much about us as about God. It is not about the fulfillment of my longings and the resolving of my fears but about my submitting to God. That is not all that Genesis or the Old Testament says about prayer. Indeed, the Old Testament more characteristically portrays prayer as a way of pressing my longings, fears, and sufferings onto God and pressing God to do something about them. But here and elsewhere it also reminds us that our relationship with God is one where, when the chips are down, we submit to the fact that God is God.

Old Testament stories rarely tell us directly about the thoughts and feelings of people. This lack seems strange to us because we are so interested in what people think and feel. The stories convey people's thoughts and feelings by describing the way people act, and when the Old Testament tells us that some-one got up early to do something, it implies being really com-mitted to it. We are inclined to assume Abraham must have gone in for some heart searching and must have talked all night with Sarah (let alone with Isaac) about this agonizing expecta-tion of God's. We want to know how Abraham knew it was God anyway and not Satan. The story reckons all that is unimport-ant, because its focus lies on Abraham's commitment and on his trust in God. "The boy and I will go over there and worship, and come back to you." What does he mean? How can they both come back, if he is to kill Isaac? Is he being economical with the truth again? Does he know what he means? Are the words out of his mouth before he has thought them through? Is he avoiding the implications of what he is to do? Or is he work-ing on the basis of knowing that God would be quite capable of resuscitating Isaac and of being unable to believe that ulti-mately God wants Isaac dead?

The same question arises when Isaac asks about the sheep for an offering. Is Abraham being economical with the truth in relation to his son, too? How could you tell your son you are about to kill him? Does Abraham know what he means? Are these words, too, out of his mouth before he has thought them through? Or does he speak in this way because he knows who God is and he is thus unable to believe that this story is going to end with his killing Isaac? And how are we to picture the scene as he binds Isaac to the makeshift **altar**? Is Isaac not struggling as he sees the short-term answer to his question? Is he not fighting his father off?

And how do we deal with not knowing the answer to those questions? After a movie, you may argue with friends about aspects of what it "meant," and one result is that we learn from such a conversation about why we see things a certain way. One advantage of the inclination in scriptural stories to refrain from telling us what people were thinking or feeling is the way they draw us in and make us think about such questions. Then by the way we answer them, we discover things about ourselves and the way we understand God and our relationship with God.

But the story's direct interest is what God is doing and what is going on between God and Abraham. When Abraham made

49

inescapably clear that he would do the terrible deed, then God stops him. The point of the test has been achieved.

GENESIS 22:11–19

Now I Know

[11]But Yahweh's aide called to him from the heavens and said, "Abraham, Abraham!" He said, "I'm here." [12]He said, "Don't reach out your hand to the boy; don't do anything to him, because I now know that you revere God; you have not withheld your son, your only son, from me." [13]Abraham looked up and saw: there, a ram caught in a thicket by its horns. Abraham went and took the ram and offered it up as a burnt offering instead of his son. [14]Abraham named that place "Yahweh sees," so that it is said today, "On Yahweh's mountain it is seen."

[15]Yahweh's aide called to Abraham a second time from the heavens [16]and said, "By myself I swear (Yahweh's proclamation) that because you have done this thing and not withheld your son, your only one, [17]I will bless you abundantly and make your offspring very numerous, so that they are like the stars in the heavens and the sand that is on the seashore. Your offspring will take over their enemies' city, [18]and all the nations on the earth will bless themselves by your offspring, because you listened to my voice." [19]Abraham then went back to his boys and they set off and went together to Beersheba. So Abraham lived at Beersheba.

In 1969, as the Vietnam war reached its peak, the Canadian Jewish poet and songwriter Leonard Cohen recorded a song about "The Story of Isaac." The first two verses imaginatively retell the story from Isaac's angle, but then the song ricochets into addressing people who are building **altars** now for the sacrifice of children. It closes, "Have mercy on our uniform, man of peace or man of war; the peacock spreads his fan." The reference to the peacock suggests a link with a poem from the First World War, Wilfred Owens's "Parable of the Young Man and the Old." It, too, begins by retelling the story from Genesis 22 but ricochets into a description of Abraham building parapets and trenches and binding Isaac with belts and straps. The angel then calls from heaven, points to "the ram of pride" caught in a thicket, and bids him sacrifice that instead. "But the old man would not so, but slew his son, and half the seed of Europe, one by one." My mother's oldest sister, who would have been a teenager just after the end of that war, used to talk about the way there simply were not enough boys to go around in Britain then. Too many had been killed.

A young friend of mine has just been deployed to Iraq. He is a chaplain, but this position does not carry exemption from the dangers of deployment. I believe that no chaplains have been killed in Iraq, but no one can guarantee that this will always be so; and chaplains do get injured and affected by the stress like combatants. Modern societies more or less accept the way countries go to war against each other and accept that their young men and women pay the biggest price for that. In theory, at least, the young men and women know that when they enlist. Perhaps the reason Isaac would not struggle was that he had analogous awareness. The Old Testament condemns the sacrifice of children, but one reason it does so is that Israelites, like other Middle Eastern peoples, did sometimes sacrifice their children, as we do in sending them off to war. Perhaps Isaac would know and accept this. Whether or not that is so, one significance of the story for people hearing it would be the implication that God does not ask for that sacrifice. God has looked the idea in the face and turned away from it. God provides for the sacrifice of a ram instead. Like many stories in the Old Testament, this story is not designed to give us an example of something we should do or might have to do (or an example of something we should not do). If anything, it is the opposite. It is an episode from the unique history of what God was doing with Abraham. It is not something that ever need be repeated.

There is an exception to that statement. The event was repeated, and that time there was no ram in the thicket. At Jesus' baptism, God said to him, "You are my Son, whom I love, with whom I am well pleased" (Mark 1:11). The words echo the ones that commission Abraham in Genesis 22 (as well as words from Psalm 2) and go on to echo the description of God's servant in Isaiah 42. They offer Jesus an understanding of his significance that is both affirming and solemn. "God did not spare his own Son, but gave him up for us all" (Romans 8:32). God put a monumentally hard demand on Abraham, but it was an expectation God was also prepared to fulfill.

But when Abraham has demonstrated that he is willing to do what eventually God will actually do, God's **aide** calls out to him, with some urgency. At the beginning of the story, Genesis told us that God spoke in person; here, the way the aide goes on to speak suggests that in effect the aide *is* God. The aide talks about "revering God" but also speaks of Abraham's not withholding his son from "me" (God). This way of relating events recurs when the Old Testament speaks about God or God's aide appearing and speaking, and it can seem confusing. What it does is both affirm the reality of God's actual speaking to Abraham and safeguard the fact that if God in the full sense spoke to a human being, then it would have an effect like the loudest thunder there could ever be; it would destroy Abraham's hearing. God really speaks but does so in muted form, as elsewhere God really appears but does so in veiled form. The aide comes to reaffirm God's promise to Abraham, in even brighter technicolor, in light of his passing his test.

Naming the mountain gives the audience several things to think about. Abraham had declared his conviction that God would see to the need for an animal to sacrifice, and God did that. So this is a place where "Yahweh sees" in the sense of looking out for people and seeing that needs are met. Abraham's name for the place also echoes Hagar's name for God as "The One Who Looks for Me" or "The One Who Sees Me." Furthermore, this mountain is located in the area of Moriah. While we do not know the actual origin of that name, it resembles words for "seeing," so the name itself would remind people that this is the place where God "saw" in that connection. And if Moriah or "Yahweh's mountain" is the mountain where the temple was, this is the place that people know as one where they and their needs are seen and attended to. Out of the context, one might translate the phrase as denoting that "On Yahweh's mountain *he* is seen." This is where God appears, where you can meet with God. The golden-domed shrine on the site of the temple in Jerusalem is placed over the site revered before Muslim times as the place where Abraham made his offering (though in Muslim tradition, it is Ishmael whom Abraham agrees to offer, and it happens in Mecca).

But why did God need to test Abraham? The story again makes us ask whether God does not know how a person like Abraham would react to a command of this kind. Sometimes tests happen for the benefit of the person being tested. If the man I referred to in relation to Genesis 20:1–13 experiences sexual temptation again and resists it, he will have learned something about himself. But this story is explicit that the testing happens so God can discover something. That was so at the beginning of the story in the reference to testing. It was so when the aide bade Abraham halt the sacrificial act: "Now I know that you revere God; you have not withheld your son, your only son, from me." The Bible ignores the logic of the question of whether God could not know how a person like Abraham would react if he had this demand placed on him. Perhaps God could indeed know how Abraham will react, but God does not relate to us and to the world by mind games played inside God's head. It is one thing to know that someone who loves you would do anything for you because of that; it is another kind of knowing when that person actually makes a monumental sacrifice for you.

GENESIS 22:20–23:20

When Your Spouse Dies

[20]Some time after this, Abraham was told, "Now. Milcah, too, has borne children to your brother Nahor: [21]Uz his firstborn, Buz his brother, Kemuel the father of Aram, [22]Chesed, Hazo, Pildash, Jidlaph, and Bethuel"; [23]Bethuel became the father of Rebekah. These eight Milcah bore Nahor, Abraham's brother. [24]His secondary wife, whose name was Reumah, also bore Tebah, Gaham, Tahash, and Maacah.

[23:1]Sarah lived to be one hundred and twenty-seven years, as the length of her life. [2]Sarah died at Kiriath Arba (that is, Hebron) in the country of Canaan. Abraham went to mourn for Sarah and to weep for her. [3]Then Abraham got up from lying on his dead wife and spoke to the Hittites: [4]"I am an alien resident with you. Give me a burial holding with you so that I may bury my dead wife away from my dwelling." ⁵The Hittites responded to Abraham by saying to him, ⁶"Hear us, my lord. You are a mighty leader among us. Bury your dead in the choicest of our burial places. None of us would withhold his burial place from you for burying your dead." ⁷Abraham got up and bowed low to the people of the country, the Hittites, ⁸and spoke with them: "If it is your desire that I should bury my wife away from my dwelling, hear me and intercede for me with Ephron son of Zohar, ⁹so that he may give me the cave at Machpelah which is his and which is at the edge of his field. May he give it to me for the full price as a burial holding among you." ¹⁰Now Ephron was sitting among the Hittites. Ephron the Hittite responded to Abraham in the ears of the Hittites, all who had come to the gate of his city: ¹¹"No, my lord, listen to me: The field—I give it to you, and the cave that is in it—I give it to you, in the sight of all my people I give it to you. Bury your dead." ¹²Abraham bowed low before the people of the country ¹³and spoke with Ephron in the ears of all the people of the country: "But if you yourself would please listen to me. I give you the price of the field. Take it from me, so that I may bury my dead there." ¹⁴Ephron responded to Abraham, saying to him, ¹⁵"My lord, listen to me: land worth four hundred shekels—between you and me, what is that? Go and bury your dead." ¹⁶Abraham listened to Ephron. Abraham weighed out to Ephron the price that he had spoken of in the ears of the Hittites, four hundred shekels of silver, as current for the merchants. ¹⁷So Ephron's field which was at Machpelah which was east of Mamre (the field and the cave that was in it and all the trees that were in the field, which were in all its borders around) passed ¹⁸to Abraham as his property in the sight of the Hittites, all who had come to the gate of his city. ¹⁹After this Abraham buried his wife Sarah in the cave in the field at Machpelah, east of Mamre (that is, Hebron) in the country of Canaan. ²⁰The field and the cave that was in it passed to Abraham as a burial holding from the Hittites.

I know where I want to bury my wife and where I want to be buried. Actually, it's rather that I know where I want our ashes to be scattered. We spent the first night of our honeymoon in a hotel in Dovedale in England (we could afford only one night), a lovely valley in the hills of Derbyshire with a stream running through it, not far from the retreat center where we first met. After breakfast, in bright sunshine we walked down the valley to a place where there were stepping stones across the stream. Ann was wearing a very short summer dress, white with a blue and green flowery pattern, which she had made. It is as well I can remember the details, because I accidentally threw away most of our honeymoon photographs, but that is another story. We eventually lived for twenty-seven years quite near Dovedale and would sometimes go there on a Saturday or Sunday with our sons, and even have lunch on the hotel's patio. So I imagine Ann dying here in the United States, and having her cremated, and taking her ashes back to England, and walking by myself down that same lane, and scattering the ashes near the stepping stones, and having tea on the hotel patio; and I hope my sons will scatter my ashes there, too. (Or maybe all that will be reversed, which will be fine.)

It is more traditional to want to have an actual burial place with a tombstone, and it is something like this that Abraham wants for Sarah. He needs to have a place that is "away from his dwelling"; he does not expect to bury Sarah in his backyard. But he wants the place to be not too far away. By implication, I presume, he wants to be buried there with her, and this is what his sons do for him in due course. The idea of a burial cave is that there is plenty of room for the whole family. When you die, you go to be with your family. So he negotiates the purchase of a cave that will work as a burial site in the area where he lives. In a broader context, the Hittites were one of the major civilizations of the Middle East in Abraham's day, but those Hittites lived in Turkey. In the Old Testament, the Hittites usually appear as one of the many ethnic groups indigenous to **Canaan** whom the Israelites eventually replace (see Genesis 15:20). Maybe these are a group of those other Hittites who had migrated to the Hebron area, or maybe they are another group with a similar name. But evidently they are the people who control the area, with whom Abraham has to negotiate the acquisition of a burial place. The story reflects the gracious etiquette of Middle Eastern community life, in which there is much polite talk among the heads of the Hittite families gathered in the plaza at the city gate, but Abraham knows he will have to pay the going price for the land if he wants actually to own it; he just has to find out what it is.

Abraham speaks as merely a resident alien in the country but ends up as the owner of a piece of land there. While the Hittites are willing to grant him a space in their burial places, Abraham wants the family to have a burial place of its own. Perhaps there is some symbolism about gaining it. The entire country is destined to belong to his offspring; this is the first piece of it that he actually owns. It then serves as a foretaste of what is to follow (though God declared the intention to give them the country, and one might wonder whether Abraham is supposed to be paying money for it).

For Sarah herself, it means she is forever at home in the country God has promised to her family. You can still visit the mausoleum erected over her burial place, on the assumption that this traditional location of the Machpelah cave is correct (it would seem reasonable that her family would make sure they stayed aware of where Sarah and Abraham were buried), and on the assumption that relationships between Israelis and Palestinians are not too fraught. Sarah deserves our remembering her. She is the great foremother of Jews and Christians (Muslim attitudes to her are naturally more equivocal because of the way she treated Hagar and Ishmael). She is this spunky woman who lived for years with the aching sadness of her childlessness, whom her husband knew he could not mess with (though he tried hard), and who was no pushover even for God. But she was a woman who eventually saw God's promises fulfilled and was able to laugh. "Look to Sarah who bore you," God later urges the people of **Judah** when they are only a shadow of their former self (Isaiah 51:2). If God could do miracles with Sarah, he can do miracles with her descendants.

The opening verses of Genesis 22:20–24 give people listening some important background to events that will follow. They concern the family "back home" in Harran, and their significance for the story will become clear in the next stage.

GENESIS 24:1–20

Where to Find Isaac a Wife

[1]So Abraham was old, advanced in years, and Yahweh had blessed Abraham in every way. [2]Abraham said to the senior servant in his household, who controlled everything that he had, "Put your hand under my thigh, [3]and I will get you to swear by Yahweh the God of heaven and the God of earth that you will not get a wife for my son from the daughters of the Canaanites among whom I am living, [4]but go to my country, to my home, and get a wife for my son Isaac." [5]The servant said to him, "Perhaps the woman will not be willing to follow me to this country: should I actually take your son back to the country that you came from?" [6]Abraham said to him, "Make sure you do not take my son back there. [7]Yahweh, the God of heaven, who took me from my father's household and from my homeland and spoke to me and swore to me, 'To your offspring I will give this country'—he will send his aide ahead of you and you will get a wife for my son from there. [8]If the woman is not willing to follow you, then you will be clear of this oath to me. Only do not take my son back there."

[9]So the servant put his hand under the thigh of his master Abraham and swore to him concerning this matter. [10]The servant took ten of his master's camels and went with all the good things belonging to his master. He set out and came to Aramnaharaim, to Nahor's city. [11]He made the camels kneel down outside the city at the well of water, at evening time, the time when the women who draw water come out. [12]He said, "Yahweh, God of my master Abraham, do make things happen for me today. Act in commitment to my master Abraham. [13]Now. I am standing by the spring of water, and the daughters of the townspeople are coming out to draw water. [14]May the girl to whom I say, 'Do put down your jar so that I can drink,' and she says 'Drink, and I will also water your camels,' may she be the one you have decided on for your servant Isaac. By this I shall acknowledge that you have acted in commitment to my master."

[15]Before he had finished speaking, there was Rebekah, who had been born to Bethuel, son of Milcah, wife of Nahor, Abraham's brother, coming out with her jar on her shoulder. [16]The girl was very beautiful in appearance, a young woman that no

one had slept with. She went down to the spring, filled her jar, and came up. [17]The servant ran to meet her and said, "Do let me sip a little water from your jar." [18]She said, "Drink, sir," and quickly lowered her jar onto her hand and let him drink. [19]When she had finished letting him drink, she said, "I will draw water for your camels as well until they have finished drinking." [20]She quickly emptied her jar into the trough, ran back to the well to draw water, and drew for all his camels.

When you make your short list of the things that you pray most concerning your children, their being able to marry the "right" person (and keep that marriage going) is near the top of the list. Our sons married beautiful, strong women whom we love and admire, and we were relieved to be able to entrust our sons to them in order that as wives they can do with them what we failed to do. I joke (maybe) that it was when we had gotten our sons into the arms of good women that we were able to flee the country. When they married, our sons were only a few years older than we had been, but the son with children sometimes speaks a little wistfully about not having enough energy for parenthood at his age. And he is only in his thirties! I read about men in their fifties or sixties marrying younger women and starting a family, and I wonder what it would be like to be in your sixties or seventies and be the father of teenagers. I also wonder what it would be like for the mother whose husband therefore likely dies before sons and daughters get married. It must be worrying, odd, and grievous having to arrange a marriage for your son or daughter when your spouse has already died. In a traditional society, people commonly marry as teenagers, as Rebekah is about to do, and your children would start marrying before you were middle-aged. But you might then die when you are quite young, as happened to one of Abraham's brothers and one of his daughters-in-law. Once again, a mother or father might have to arrange a marriage without the involvement of a partner.

In a sense, this situation raises easier questions in the West, where we leave the decision about whom to marry to the people who are least likely to make a sensible decision. (My prospective father-in-law so disapproved of me that he threatened not to come to the wedding, but it did not make Ann and me think about terminating the relationship.) In a traditional society such as Abraham's, he has to take responsibility for the matter. He, too, has to do so on his own as a result of Sarah's having Isaac in her old age (whatever that would mean in "real" figures). In such a society, it is customary to marry someone from outside your household but inside your extended family (though "extended family" means something rather more extended than it means in the West). In large part, it is a matter of practicality, concerning not eugenics but relationships. Marrying someone inside the household is just too disturbing to the household's way of working and relating. On the other hand, Israelites typically lived in villages comprising two or three households that could trace their interrelationships to common family origins. (Abraham's own story illustrates how such a household would be larger than Westerners would think of as a household—in fact, not so different from what Westerners might think of as an extended family. In a village, they would occupy a number of actual households, but all under one head.) The natural place to find a wife or husband is one of the other households in the village.

Abraham's problem is that his household is separated from the other households in his broader family or clan, so he needs to send "back home" for a wife for Isaac. The story provides no rationale for this; it is just "obvious" that this is what you would do, as it is "obvious" in a Western context that young men and women find their own partners and that their parents may discover who it is only when the arrangements are cut and dried.

Abraham's strong insistence about Isaac's not marrying someone from among the **Canaanites** nuances all this. It would ring bells for people listening to Genesis, in whose context the Canaanites are people practicing a religion that often attracts Israelites and influences them in a way that "proper" Old Testament faith disapproves of. We have noted one instance, the way Middle Eastern religion could approve of the sacrifice of a child when the **Torah** and the Prophets do not. Western thinking keeps ethnic considerations and religious considerations in separate compartments, at least in theory, but this is another of those oddities of our particular culture. Usually ethnic considerations and religious ones are mixed up. On the surface in this story, Isaac's not marrying a Canaanite girl is a cultural and ethnic principle, but it also presupposes a religious principle. A Canaanite spouse will lead you into Canaanite ways.

It is particularly vital that this does not happen to Isaac and that he marry the right kind of girl, because he is the one through whom God intends to bring blessing to the world. Paradoxically, he has to stay separate from the world in order to be a blessing to it. So it is not mere chronological precision that makes this Genesis's last story about Abraham. Making sure Isaac marries the right kind of girl is Abraham's last significant act. After that, he can die. His work is done. This also explains why Abraham can be absolutely confident about God's ensuring that his **aide**'s search will be successful. God's own plan depends on it.

These considerations also link with Abraham's insistence that the servant not take Isaac himself back to Abraham's homeland. Being in the country is tied up with the fulfillment of that purpose. Leaving the country would involve a kind of going back on God's purpose. It becomes necessary for Jacob and for Jacob's family, though the reasons for and the consequences of that are not happy.

GENESIS 24:21–48

How to Find Isaac a Wife

²¹The man was looking at her, staying quiet, to know whether or not Yahweh had made his journey successful. ²²When the camels had finished drinking, the man got a gold nose-ring (its weight a half-shekel) and two gold bracelets (their weight ten shekels). ²³He said, "Whose daughter are you? Do tell me. Is there room at your father's house for us to stay the night?" ²⁴She said to him, "I am the daughter of Bethuel, son of Milcah, whom she bore Nahor." ²⁵She said to him, "There is plenty of both straw and fodder there, and also a place to stay the night." ²⁶The man fell down and bowed low to Yahweh ²⁷and said, "Yahweh the God of my master Abraham be praised, who did not abandon his commitment and his steadfastness toward my master. I myself—Yahweh has led me on the way to the house

of my master's relatives." [28]The girl ran and told her mother's household all these things that had happened.

[29]Now Rebekah had a brother named Laban, and Laban ran out to the spring to the man. [30]When he saw the nose-ring and his sister's two bracelets and heard the words of his sister Rebekah saying, "This is how the man spoke to me," he went to the man. There he was, standing by the camels by the well. [31]He said, "Come in, you who are blessed by Yahweh. Why stand outside when I have made the house ready, with a place for the camels?" [32]So the man went into the house and unharnessed the camels. He gave the camels straw and fodder, and water to wash his feet and the feet of the men who were with him. [33]Something to eat was set before him. But he said, "I will not eat until I have spoken my words." So he said, "Speak."

[34]He said, "I am Abraham's servant. [35]As Yahweh has greatly blessed my master, he has become a great man. He has given him sheep and cattle, silver and gold, male and female servants, camels and donkeys. [36]Sarah, my master's wife, bore my master a son in her old age, and he has given him everything that he has. [37]My master got me to swear, saying, 'You will not get a wife for my son from the daughters of the Canaanites among whom I am living in their country, [38]but go to my father's household, to my kin, and get a wife for my son.' [39]I said to my master, 'Perhaps the woman will not follow me.' [40]He said to me, 'Yahweh, before whom I have walked—he will send his aide with you and he will make your journey successful. You will get a wife for my son from my kin. [41]Then you will be free from my oath if, when you come to my kin, they do not give her to you. You will be free from my oath.'

[42]I came today to the spring and I said, 'Yahweh, God of my master Abraham: If you could indeed be one who grants success to my journey that I am making! [43]Now, I am standing by the spring of water. May the girl who comes out to draw and to whom I say, "Could you let me drink a little water from your jar," [44]and she says to me, "Drink, and I will also draw for your camels," may she be the woman whom Yahweh has decided on for my master's son.' [45]Before I had finished speaking in my heart, there was Rebekah coming out with her jar on her shoulder. She went down to the spring and drew. I said to her, 'Could you give me a drink?' [46]She quickly lowered her jar from on her shoulder and said, 'Drink, and I will water your camels as well.'

So I drank, and she watered the camels as well. [47]I asked her, 'Whose daughter are you?' and she said, 'The daughter of Bethuel, the son of Nahor, whom Milcah bore him.' And I put the ring on her nose and the bracelets on her arms. [48]I fell down and bowed low to Yahweh and praised Yahweh the God of my father Abraham, who had led me on the right way to get the daughter of my master's brother for his son.'"

The first of the "Four Spiritual Laws" that have been the starting point for many people coming to faith in Christ is that "God loves you and offers a wonderful plan for your life." The law is supported by scriptural verses affirming God's love and God's desire that we might have life and have it abundantly. Yet somehow, in spelling out the implications of this law, people often infer that it means that God has a detailed plan for what school one should go to and what job one should do—and for whom to marry. I make myself unpopular with my students sometimes by suggesting that there is no indication of this in the Bible (and that it would be odd, because God is a loving Father, and truly loving fathers do not have plans for how their children should live their lives). Yet sometimes God does have such a plan for an individual's life because there is a particular role God wants that person to fulfill. Moses is an example, and so is Jeremiah (and they illustrate how God's plan for a person's life is quite likely to be unwelcome). So is Abraham, and so is Isaac.

The servant assumes God does have a plan regarding whom Isaac should marry and he goes about his commission in light of that conviction. He sets off for Aram-naharaim, "**Aram** of the two rivers," the area where Harran is, and he prays an insanely bold prayer. It is not the kind of prayer you could regularly expect to have answered, but he prays to "the God of my master Abraham" and he is able to challenge God to manifest **commitment** to Abraham (the word comes three times on the servant's lips). God has made promises to Abraham about the significance of his son, so the servant can pray with boldness on the basis of those promises.

Isaac's special place in God's purpose means that we cannot all expect to pray the servant's kind of prayer and have confidence it will be answered (though we can pray the servant's kind of prayer and hope it might be answered). In this sense there is no great encouragement for ordinary mortals in this story. In another sense there is greater encouragement than we might have realized, because its implication is that when the issue is the fulfillment of God's purpose for the world (including for us as ordinary mortals), God can be trusted to come through. Jesus once told his disciples that if they asked for anything in his name, they would receive it (John 14:14). It is a puzzling promise. For many people, it does not work to ask in Jesus' name for someone's healing or for a job when you are made redundant. But maybe "in Jesus' name" implies "as something that is or could be part of the achievement of God's purpose in the world." And that kind of prayer does get answered.

So Abraham gets the servant to swear that he will do what Abraham says. Putting his hand under Abraham's thigh and thus in contact with his genitals in some way undergirds the solemnity of the oath (we do not know exactly why it did that). Given that the commission is such an important one, it is striking that Abraham will entrust it to a mere "servant," and it shows what a responsible and honored position a "servant" or "slave" (the same word) can occupy. The way the servant goes about his task shows how well-founded was Abraham's trust in him. He knows how to pray, and he knows how to be silent and watch and wait, and he knows how to worship and give honor to the God who has answered his crazy prayer, and he knows how to keep his mission in mind even when social custom would oblige him to accept hospitality and not do anything that looks like business until much later. There are times to live by social custom and times to flout it.

This servant is important, yet we do not get to know his name because his importance lies in what he does. Perhaps he therefore does not mind that we do not know his name. No paparazzi follow him. But he is indeed someone "blessed by **Yahweh**." Perhaps Laban does not know his name, and this phrase is merely a polite greeting, but the prominence of the theme of blessing in the Abraham story means that the people listening to the story know the greeting points to something significant. The chapter began by noting how God had blessed Abraham, and the servant now tells the tale Genesis has already told us, beginning with the way "Yahweh has greatly blessed my master." Being associated with the person God blesses and being involved in the fulfillment of God's purpose that is tied up with him means he himself has received blessing. He wasn't seeking it. He was just doing his job.

GENESIS 24:49–25:6

The First Romance?

[49]"So now: if you are going to act with commitment and steadfastness to my master, tell me. And if not, tell me, so that I may turn right or left." [50]Laban and Bethuel answered, "It is from Yahweh that the matter has come forth. We cannot speak to you bad or good. [51]There is Rebekah in front of you. Take her and go and she can be a wife for your master's son, as Yahweh has said." [52]When Abraham's servant heard their words, he bowed low to the ground before Yahweh. [53]The servant brought out objects of silver and objects of gold, and garments, and gave them to Rebekah, and gave presents to her brother and her mother. [54]They ate and drank, he and the men who were with him, and spent the night. They got up in the morning, and he said, "Send me off to my master." [55]Her brother and her mother said, "The girl should stay with us for (say) ten days. After, you can go." [56]He said to them, "Don't make me delay when Yahweh has made my journey successful. Send me off so I can go to my master." [57]They said, "We will call the girl and ask her what she says." [58]So they called Rebekah and said to her, "Will you go with this man?" She said, "I will go." [59]So they sent their sister Rebekah off, with her nanny and Abraham's servant and his men. [60]They blessed Rebekah and said to her, "Our sister, may you grow to be thousands of myriads, and may your offspring take possession of their enemies' city." [61]And Rebekah and her girls got up and mounted their camels and followed the man.

So the servant took Rebekah and went. [62]Now Isaac had come from going to Beer-lahai-roi; he was living was in the Negev region. [63]Isaac had gone out to walk and think in the countryside toward evening, and he looked up and saw: there were camels coming. [64]Rebekah looked up and saw Isaac. She jumped off her camel [65]and said to the servant, "Who is that man walking in the countryside about to meet us?" The servant said,

"That is my master." She took her veil and covered herself, [66]and the servant told Isaac all that he had done. [67]So Isaac brought her into the tent of his mother Sarah. He took Rebekah, and she became his wife, and he loved her. So Isaac found consolation after his mother's death.

[25:1]Abraham again took a wife, whose name was Keturah. [2]She bore him Zimran, Jokshan, Medan, Midian, Ishbak, and Shuah. [3]Jokshan was the father of Sheba and Dedan, while the descendants of Dedan were the Asshurites, the Letushites, and the Leummites, [4]and the descendants of Midian were Ephah, Epher, Enoch, Abida, and Eldaah. All these were descendants of Keturah. [5]Abraham gave all that he had to Isaac, [6]but to the sons of Abraham's secondary wives Abraham gave gifts while he was still alive and sent them off away from his son Isaac eastward, to the east country.

Ann and I were sitting in a restaurant waiting for dinner to arrive. There should have been jazz, but the restaurant had been busted by the city authorities for not having a music license, so it was quiet, and I was reading to Ann from Barack Obama's memoir, *The Audacity of Hope*. Suddenly to my astonishment (and making me start to weep) I read that his father-in-law had multiple sclerosis, the disease that has disabled Ann. In Frasier Robinson's case, the disease was diagnosed when he was thirty; for the next twenty-five years as he battled on manfully, he and his family lived "carefully circumscribed" lives, "with even the smallest outing carefully planned to avoid problems or awkwardness" (we could identify with all that). Eventually he died when he was fifty-five, and Obama describes watching his casket lower into the ground and promising to take care of Mr. Robinson's girl (they were not yet married).

Maybe there is a sense in which for anyone who gets married, one's partner takes the place of one's parents. It was so for Isaac.

First, once again the servant talks about **commitment**, but now the question concerns not God's commitment but that of Bethuel and Laban. The question is whether they still feel a family commitment to Abraham despite his having parted from the family decades ago. If the answer is "No," the servant will have to look elsewhere. But they recognize they have no right to behave as if the decision is theirs. God has already made it. Their little daughter and little sister (she will be no more than a teenager) has been hoisted into that purpose of God, whether they like it or not—like Moses, Jeremiah, Jonah, Saul on the Damascus road, and Abraham himself. Of course in theory you may have opportunity to say, "No" (though quite likely God will not accept your refusal, to judge from those examples). So once again the servant bows in worship to the God who continues to make his mission successful. And with the important business done, proprieties can be given their place, and hospitality, accepted.

Err. . . . What about Rebekah's view on the matter? It seems that her destiny is being decided by a crowd of men. As we already know from Sarah, in Isaac and Rebekah's story it will turn out that a woman knows how to find her way in a patriarchal world and that her simple cooperation with men's projects cannot be taken for granted. In this story it may be only for dramatic effect that the question of Rebekah's acquiescence in God's plans is raised only the next day. "I'll go," she says.

We do not know exactly what Isaac was doing when the camel train reached Beersheba; the single word I have translated "walk and think" comes only here, though it looks like a cross between a word for "roam about" and a word for "meditate." There follows a moment a little like the one where Tony and Maria see each other across a room in *West Side Story*, with Rebekah then falling off her camel (the usual meaning of the verb). Once again the story combines propriety (she had been set up for this meeting by other people, and now she covers herself with a veil because Isaac must not see her yet) with humanity (they marry and fall in love). The order of events seems odd to Western thinking, but it corresponds to the testimony of some people who are used to marriages being arranged (though Isaac and Rebekah will not exactly live happily ever after, any more than people do by the Western arrangement).

There must be a sense in which Isaac and his family become a new family for Rebekah and make up for her being wrenched away from her birth family, whom she will never see again. Barack Obama promised to look after Frasier Robinson's daughter, but he also testifies to Michelle Robinson's family life giving him an experience of family such as he never had. What the Genesis story observes is the way Rebekah becomes the person who brings healing to the grief of Isaac's mother's death when he is himself presumably no more than a teenager.

We do not know about the chronology of Abraham's third marriage. In the story, the interest lies in its enabling Israelites to know how they relate to people such as Midian, Sheba, and Dedan, who appear on the fringe of the Old Testament story, and other peoples that are just names to us but might also have been familiar to people listening to the story, as tribes on the fringe of their lives. While the definition of a "secondary wife" may have meant that Keturah's children had no inheritance rights, Abraham nevertheless gives them a share in the family inheritance before he dies but gives the expected primary recognition to Isaac, "his only son."

GENESIS 25:7–22

Brothers United and Divided

[7]This is the sum of the years of the life that Abraham lived: one hundred and seventy-five years. [8]So he breathed his last. Abraham died at a good age, old and satisfied, and joined his kin. [9]His sons Isaac and Ishmael buried him in the cave at Machpelah in the field of Ephron son of Zohar the Hittite, which was east of Mamre, [10]the field that Abraham got from the Hittites. There Abraham and his wife Sarah were buried. [11]After Abraham's death, God blessed his son Isaac. Isaac lived near Beer-lahai-roi.

[12]This is the line of descent of Abraham's son Ishmael, whom Hagar the Egyptian, Sarah's maidservant, bore Abraham. [13]These are the names of Ishmael's sons, by their names in the order of their birth: Nebaioth, Ishmael's firstborn, Kedar, Adbeel, Mibsam, [14]Mishma, Dumah, Massa, [15]Hadad, Tema, Jetur, Naphish, and Kedemah. [16]These are Ishmael's sons and these are their names, by their settlements and by their camps, twelve leaders belonging to their peoples. [17]These are the years of the life of Ishmael: one hundred and thirty-seven years. So he breathed his last and died, and joined his kin. ([18]They dwelt from Havilah to Shur, which is east of Egypt, as you come to Asshur. He settled over against all his brothers.)

> [19]This is the line of descent of Abraham's son Isaac. Abraham fathered Isaac, [20]and when Isaac was forty years old he took for himself as wife Rebekah, daughter of Bethuel the Aramean of Paddan-aram, sister of Laban the Aramean. [21]Isaac pleaded with Yahweh in behalf of his wife because she was infertile. Yahweh responded to his pleading, and his wife Rebekah became pregnant. [22]The children pressed on one another inside her, and she said, "If this is how it is, why am I like this?" and she went to inquire of Yahweh.

Not so many years ago, my wife and I were part of a regulation three-generation family. My mother, our only surviving parent, was at the top. We were in the middle. Our sons and their wives were at the bottom. Then, within two years, my mother died and we acquired a grandchild, so that suddenly we were at the top, our sons and their wives were in the middle, with our grandchild (now, grandchildren) at the bottom. This made me think about the fact that (in terms of sociobiology) my job was done. I can die now. It was my job to have children and play my part in ensuring that the human species will continue, and I have done it now. I can leave the future to the next generation and the one after that. I can die satisfied with my life. More recently I have signed a contract to write a book series titled The Old Testament for Everyone, and I would now like to live to complete it; otherwise I will look stupid.

I am glad that my death will not be my end, and that after a sleep of indeterminate length I shall rise on resurrection day, but if this were not going to be so, for myself I would not be too bothered. Genesis assumes that Abraham is content to begin his big sleep. He goes to join his family. (The Old Testament elsewhere makes clear that people who die before their time are entitled to a different attitude, and I take a different attitude on behalf of my wife, whose life has been so constricted by her disability; I am glad she will dance on resurrection day, and I look forward to joining her.)

Abraham knows that his job is done. He and Sarah have had a son, who has grown up, and Abraham has made sure he has the right wife. Although she has not had a baby yet, Abraham knows that God can sort that out and that he can entrust the future of God's promise to God and to Isaac now. It is through him that God's purpose is going to be fulfilled.

At the same time, it is neat to picture Ishmael and Isaac together burying their father. Death in the family is one of those occasions when the tensions all come out, and one could not blame Ishmael if he felt put out at the way God has given Isaac priority over him and the way Abraham has done the same in not treating him as his real son when it matters—in his will (see the opening verses of Genesis 25). But Ishmael is a big man. There he is, joining Isaac in burying their father.

His secondary significance comes out again in the way Genesis goes on to provide an account of his descendants. As happens in Genesis 1–11, the line mentioned first comes there in order to be cleared out of the way before the story comes to the line that really matters. Once again, the account provides the audience with a framework for understanding the position of people who live around them, desert peoples we know of from elsewhere in the Old Testament, such as Kedar and Dumah, and other peoples we know nothing about. The paragraph makes more explicit than some earlier lists that they are talking about individuals who also stand for the groups that trace their ancestry back to them, as "**Israel**" traces itself back to "Israel." The last comment on Ishmael that he "settled" over against his wider family suggests a fulfillment of the prophecy or promise God's **aide** gave his mother (Genesis 16:12). More literally he "fell" in the sense of "leapt," like Rebekah jumping off her camel (Genesis 24:64). Like Genesis 16, Genesis 25 indicates that Ishmael is a survivor. No one knocks him over. If he falls, he falls on his feet.

It is both paradoxical and logical that Genesis doesn't have so much to tell us about Abraham once he has had his son (there's just Sarah's death and the arranging of Isaac's marriage) and that the first thing it tells us about Isaac concerns how he and Rebekah come to have children. That's what the fulfilling of God's purpose depends on. Like Isaac's parents and many others in Genesis and elsewhere, Isaac and Rebekah have trouble starting a family, and like other such would-be parents, getting pregnant is then only the beginning of their problems. What's distinctive about Isaac and Rebekah is the way they react to all that. First, it makes Isaac pray. The word Genesis uses is not one that appears often. It is used mostly in connection with Moses praying for God to take away the afflictions God brings on the Egyptians, but it also comes in the context of some other illnesses and afflictions. So it suggests laying hold of God to remove some disaster. It will indeed be a disaster if Isaac and Rebekah cannot have children. Typically, the story assumes that the problem lies in Rebekah. Often this assumption may be justified by the fact that when the man tries with another wife, as Abraham did, she gets pregnant. In other cases, such as this one, it might be that the problem lies in Isaac. But God deals with it anyway.

More distinctive is the next round of prayer, which follows. Like other women in these stories, such as Sarah and Rachel, Rebekah is not the kind of person who just sits at home demurely submitting to her husband and accepting her lot. She takes action. At this point she does so by assuming that she too can talk to God about what the heck is going on. She does not have to leave prayer to her husband or go to God via him as if she had no relationship with God of her own. She has the freedom the Psalms illustrate to go straight to God with the issues in her life. In a context where there are no convenient ob-gyn clinics, getting pregnant is a good way to die, and feeling such stressful events taking place inside her would be very scary (one of her daughters-in-law will die in childbirth). Precisely how she went about inquiring of God we don't know. If this were a story from later Israel, we would infer that she went to a sanctuary and that God responded to her by means of someone like a prophet. Maybe something like this happened. What the story does make clear is the simple possibility of taking issues to God and getting a response, though the story does not establish that you get a response every time. Every Israelite woman listening to the story would know that. But it does establish that it can happen and it is therefore worth trying.

GENESIS 25:23‒26:5

Two Guys Who Need Their Heads Banged Together

[23]Yahweh said to her, "Two nations are in your womb, two peoples will separate from your body. One people will be stronger than the other people, and the elder will serve the younger." [24]The time came for her to give birth, and there: twins were in her womb. [25]The first came out all red like a "hairy" garment. They called him Esau. [26]After that, his brother came out, his hand "grasping" Esau's heel. They called him Jacob. Isaac was sixty years old when they were born.

[27]The boys grew up and Esau became a man who knew about hunting, a man of the open country, while Jacob was an upright man, staying at the tents. [28]Isaac loved Esau because of his taste for game, while Rebekah loved Jacob. [29]Jacob cooked stew, and Esau came in from the country. He was famished. [30]Esau said to Jacob, "Do stuff me with the 'red' stuff, this red stuff, because I'm famished"; hence he was called Edom. [31]Jacob said, "Sell me your birthright today." [32]Esau said, "Okay, I'm about to die. What use is a birthright to me?" [33]Jacob said, "Swear it to me today." So he swore it to him. He sold his birthright to Jacob, [34]and Jacob gave Esau bread and lentil stew. He ate and drank, and got up and went. So Esau despised the birthright.

[26:1]There was a famine in the country, besides the previous famine that happened in the days of Abraham. Isaac went to Gerar, to Abimelech, king of the Philistines. [2]Yahweh appeared to him and said, "Don't go down to Egypt. Stay in the country that I am telling you about. [3]Reside in this country. I will be with you and I will bless you, because I will give you and your offspring all these countries. I will fulfill the oath that I swore to your father Abraham. [4]I will make your offspring as numerous as the stars in the heavens, and I will give your offspring all these countries, and all the nations on earth will bless themselves by your offspring, [5]inasmuch as Abraham listened to my voice and kept my charge, my commands, and my instructions."

There's a weird thing about babies (well, many weird things). I often reflected on our having two sons, born of the same mother and father, more or less brought up in the same way by the same parents, who turned out as very different people, even from birth. Within humanity in general, there are people who always want to be number one, and people who couldn't care less. There are people who want to be president, or have a hit record, or win a TV competition, or be their parents' favorite child, or be top of the class, or get into the *Guinness Book of Records*, or write a best-selling novel (or theology book). Then there are people who couldn't care less, have no ambitions, have no great accomplishments on their vita, have no game plan for their lives; they are people who just muddle along. One is not better than the other. Both can be a danger to themselves and to other people. Their ambition or their lethargy may mean they ruin their own lives or fall short of what they could be, and/or that they fail to serve other people because of their self-concern. Ecclesiastes would look with scorn on both of them; they either overestimate achievement or underestimate it.

Jacob and Esau embody the two types. Apparently they were dizygotic, nonidentical twins, as opposed to monozygotic, identical twins. In other words, as sometimes happens with medical procedures, Isaac's prayer had been spectacularly effective in making God unlock Rebekah's womb; two of her ova were fertilized. You could tell they embodied the two types from their earliest beginnings. Esau was number one, but he wasn't bothered by that. Jacob was number two, but he always wanted to be number one. They were twins, and Esau was the older, just by a few seconds, but it was as if Jacob was already reaching out to catch up with his big brother as they left Rebekah's womb. His name says it: it means "He grasps." (The name could also mean "[God] protects," and perhaps this meaning is also suggested.) It is odd that he is described as upright, since this is not one of the first six adjectives that one would attach to Jacob in light of his story.

The story's listeners know how to understand God's explanation of what was happening in Rebekah's womb a few weeks earlier, because they themselves are Jacob. Although Jacob eventually gets the new name Israel, which is his descendants' regular name, the Old Testament also continues to refer to the people as Jacob. Likewise Esau gets the new name Edom, which is the name of the people living just south and east of Israel who often contend with **Israel** for territory. For much of the time, Jacob-Israel will be the bigger of these two peoples.

This is a little odd. The big brother is supposed to be the senior brother. Yet precisely because it is the regular social custom, God likes to make things work the opposite way so that big brothers eventually get pushed out of the way by little brothers (think of Joseph or David).

As there was a significance in Jacob's birth name and in his new name, so it is with Esau, and more so. First, **Esau** is quite close to the word for hair; hence the reference to Esau looking like a hairy garment. It implies that he is a rough-looking guy, a guy who will be at home in the wild. His personality and destiny, like Jacob's, seemed to be announced in the way he was when he was born. His hairiness was not the only aspect of his birth that Rebekah remembered. He also came out all red; and "red" is even closer to the name "Edom" than "hair" is to Esau. So this will be a story about Grabber and Red. But the story waits to make explicit that Esau gained this second name, until it tells us about the red lentil stew that Esau was so eager to eat.

Presumably Esau was exaggerating when he said he was starving, dying of hunger; at least, that was always the case with our two sons. And he wasn't bothered about being number one. If that was so important—well, let Jacob have the birthright. Who cares, when what you need is something to eat? Jacob cares. When you need to be number one and you are not number one, you care deeply. You will do anything to get there. But Jacob didn't have to do much—just cook a pot of stew at the right moment.

The uneasy relationship between Isaac's sons, harbingering an uneasy relationship between the peoples who trace their descent to them, is not the only parallel between Isaac's story and his father's story (it has the effect of suggesting Isaac never did anything interesting or have anything interesting happen to him; he just fills the space between Abraham and Jacob). As with Abraham, God appears to Isaac and promises that he will become a numerous people and will (at least through them) come to possess the country and be a standard for people's prayer for blessing. Like Abraham, Isaac has to cope with famine, and also like Abraham, he takes refuge in Gerar in the territory of a king called Abimelech (presumably a different one). The parallels will continue as that story unfolds.

Yet there are noteworthy distinctive features of God's words to Isaac. One is the prohibition on going to Egypt, recalling Abraham's command to his servant not to have Isaac leave the country in the other direction in order to find a wife. *This* is the promised land. Don't leave it even under pressure. There is the related promise, "I will be with you." God was certainly with Abraham, as Abimelech could see (Genesis 21:22), but God did not express an actual commitment to Abraham in these terms. So one could call this the Isaac promise (it will be repeated for other people, and for Israel itself, but it starts off as the Isaac promise). God's being with Isaac does not merely mean that Isaac has a sense of God's being there through tough times, or even that God actually is with Isaac through tough times whether or not Isaac has a sense of it. In the Bible, God's being with you is something that makes a practical difference to how things work out. So when external circumstances seem to be working against you, God's being with you will issue in blessing (fruitfulness and flourishing). Paradoxically that will be true because Isaac's father did what God said by being prepared to kill Isaac! Abraham's commitment to treating Isaac as dispensable is the basis for God's commitment to blessing Isaac. The attitude that parents have to their children, to God, and the way they see the relationship between these two attitudes can have profound implications for the way God deals with the children.

GENESIS 26:6–33

Do We Ever Learn?—Take Two

[6]So Isaac lived in Gerar. [7]The people in the place asked about his wife, and he said, "She is my sister," because he was afraid to say "My wife" in case "the people in the place slay me because of Rebekah, because she looks attractive." [8]But when he had been there some time, Abimelech king of the Philistines looked down from a window and saw: there was Isaac playing about with his wife Rebekah. [9]Abimelech summoned Isaac and said, "Now. Really she is your wife! How did you come to say, 'She is my sister'?" Isaac said to him, "I thought, 'In case I die because of her.'" [10]Abimelech said, "What is this that you have done to

us? Almost, someone from the people could have slept with your wife and brought guilt upon us." [11]Abimelech charged the entire people, "Anyone who touches this man or his wife will definitely be put to death."

[12]Isaac sowed in that country, and that year reaped a hundredfold. Yahweh blessed him. [13]The man grew big, and went on doing so, until he had grown very big indeed. [14]He had livestock, flocks and herds, and a large body of servants, and the Philistines were jealous of him. [15]All the wells that his father's servants had dug in the time of his father Abraham, the Philistines stopped up and filled with dirt. [16]And Abimelech said to Isaac, "Get away from us, because you are much too powerful for us."

[17]So Isaac went from there and encamped in the Gerar wash and lived there. [18]Isaac again dug the wells of water that they had dug in the time of his father Abraham and that the Philistines had stopped up after Abraham's death. He called them by the same names as his father had called them. [19]Isaac's servants dug in the wash and found there a well of spring water, [20]and the Gerar shepherds argued with Isaac's shepherds, saying, "The water is ours." He called the well "Contention" because they contended with him. [21]They dug another well and they argued over it, too, so he called it "Opposition." [22]He moved from there and dug another well, and they did not argue over it, so he called it "Roominess" and said, "Now Yahweh has given us room and we will be fruitful in the country."

[23]From there he went up to Beersheba. [24]Yahweh appeared to him that night and said, "I am the God of your father Abraham. Do not be afraid, because I will be with you, and I will bless you and make your offspring numerous on account of my servant Abraham." [25]He built an altar there and called in Yahweh's name, and pitched his tents there. Isaac's servants dug a well there. [26]Abimelech came to him from Gerar with Ahuzzath his adviser and Phicol his army commander. [27]Isaac said to them, "Why have you come to me, when you have been hostile to me and you sent me off from you?" [28]They said, "We have seen clearly that Yahweh was with you, so we said, 'There does need to be a sworn agreement between us,' between us and you. So we want to seal a covenant with you [29]that you will not do harm to us, as we have not touched you and as we have done nothing but good to you, and sent you off in peace. You are now one blessed by Yahweh." [30]So Isaac made a banquet for them, and

they ate and drank. [31]Early in the morning they swore oaths, each to the other, and Isaac sent them off and they departed from him in peace. [32]That day, Isaac's servants came and told him about the matter of a well that they had dug, and said to him, "We have found water." [33]He called it "Shibah." Hence the name of the city is Beersheba until this day.

A few weeks ago, the great U.S. novelist John Updike died. I think I had tried to read one of his novels years ago but failed. In light of the eulogies, I thought I should try again, so I started with *Too Far to Go*, over which one of the eulogies enthused. It is actually a collection of short stories about a married couple called Richard and Joan Maple. They have a strangely dysfunctional and codependent relationship. I happened last night to be reading a story in which they are telling each other about their affairs. The story is mostly told from Richard's angle; at least we get more insight into what is going through his mind than into what is going through Joan's. A striking feature of the story is Richard's strange fascination with his wife's affairs and her lovers. He wants to know how many there have been and how many times she has met with them and where. . . . He does not seem to be repelled by all this. He is drawn into it.

It reminded me of a comment on the stories about Abraham and Isaac and their wives. It is neat that Genesis here speaks of Isaac's "playing about" with Rebekah, because the verb is the one linked to Isaac's own name, the verb that kept coming in Genesis 17–21 with the meaning "laugh." Isaac was being himself in making out with Rebekah. So this story about Isaac and his wife is told in a distinctive way. But the occurrence of another story like the ones about Abraham and Sarah raises the question of why these men were so stupid. Did they never learn? Further, why does Genesis include three of these stories about someone passing on his wife as his sister and risking her ending up in the king's bed? There were surely many other stories Genesis could have included. Maybe the answer is that men can have a strange ambivalence about their wives' sexuality. Like Richard Maple, we want our wives to be ours, but there is also something intriguing about other men wanting our wives. It is a kind of compliment. There is no way of knowing whether this was a conscious motivation for the inclusion of these stories in Genesis; it might have been only a subconscious one (or not even that). Whatever is the answer to that question, the stories can now function to make men reflect on their subconscious thinking and make women aware of it, too. Indeed, in the West the sexual politics often need to be seen both ways, so the stories might encourage women to reflect on their own subconscious thinking about their husbands, and husbands to be aware of it.

In extraordinary contrast with the account of Isaac's stupidity, Genesis goes on to describe how well Isaac did in Abimelech's country. Now, your mother probably told you that if you behaved well, things would work out well for you, and (more important) if you behave badly, you will pay for it. Often that's true, but often it isn't. God doesn't seem to view it as important to be fair (rather than saying God is fair, Jesus notes that God makes the sun shine and the rain fall on both righteous and unrighteous, which probably isn't what your mother told you). The question of fairness and unfairness is subordinate to other priorities. In Genesis the priority is God's making Abraham and his offspring an embodiment of God's blessing that will attract the world, and Isaac's story illustrates that purpose at work. Actually, blessing Isaac when he doesn't deserve it is an important expression of something about God that might be expected to attract people, even if it would worry your mother. The Old Testament God operates on the basis of grace rather than merit. The more pathetic the characters in the stories are (and they can be pretty pathetic), the clearer becomes this gospel principle.

We have mixed feelings about this biblical motif, because it makes our lives less subject to calculation and control. Abimelech and his people certainly had mixed feelings about it. One issue in whose context it surfaces is water supply. The Negev area where these stories are located (Beersheba, Beer-lahai-roi, Gerar) is close to being desert; Beersheba gets about ten days of rain per year. That raises tough questions about whether anyone could live there. But there is water under the ground, and digging wells thus makes living there possible. Digging wells, however, can require huge amounts of manpower, so once wells have been dug, they can become matters of dispute.

The song notes that it never rains in Southern California, but "they never warn you how it pours" when the rains do come (I never needed galoshes in England). The Middle East can be similar. A wash is the bed of a river that flows only when there has been a storm (in Arabic it is a **wadi**; in Hebrew, a **nahal**). Living there has its dangers; you need to keep your eye open for the storms that could wash away you and your encampment. But when the rains do come, you can trap some water, and when they have gone, grass will grow for your flocks.

GENESIS 26:34–27:33

How Stupid Parents Can Be

[34]When Esau was forty years old, he took as wife Judith, the daughter of Beeri the Hittite, and Basemath, the daughter of Elon the Hittite, [35]but they produced a bitterness of spirit in Isaac and Rebekah.

[27:1]When Isaac was old and his eyes were too dim to see, he called his elder son Esau and said to him, "Son!" Esau said to him, "I'm here." [2]Isaac said, "Well, I'm old. I don't know when I shall die. [3]So now, will you pick up your equipment, your quiver and your bow, and go out into the open country, and hunt game for me. [4]Make me a dish the way I like, and bring it to me to eat, and I will give you my personal blessing before I die." [5](Rebekah was listening when Isaac spoke to his son Esau.) So Esau went into the country to hunt game to bring home, [6]and Rebekah said to her son Jacob, "Right: I heard your father speaking to your brother Esau, saying, [7]'Bring me game and make me a dish to eat and I will bless you before Yahweh before I die.' [8]But now, son, listen to what I say, to what I am telling you. [9]Go to the flock and get me two choice kid goats from there, and I'll make them into a dish for your father, the way he likes, [10]and you can take it to your father to eat, so he may bless you before he dies." [11]Jacob said to his mother Rebekah, "Well. My brother Esau is a hairy man and I am a smooth-skinned man. [12]Suppose my father touches me, and sees I am tricking him. I shall bring on myself belittling not blessing." [13]His mother said to him, "Your belittling be on me, son. Just listen to what I say. Go and get them for me." [14]So he went and got them and brought them to his mother, and his mother made a dish the way his father liked. [15]Rebekah got her elder son Esau's clothes, the best ones, which were with her in the house, and put them on her younger son Jacob. [16]The skin of the kid goats she put on his hands and on the smooth part of his neck, [17]and she handed her son Jacob the dish and the bread that she had made. [18]He went to his father and said, "Father!" He said, "I'm here. Who are you, son?" [19]Jacob said to his father, "I'm Esau, your firstborn. I have done as you told me. Do sit up and eat some of the game, so that you may give me your personal blessing." [20]Isaac said to his son, "How were you so quick to find it, son?" He said, "Because Yahweh your God brought it about for me." [21]Isaac said to Jacob, "Do draw near so I can feel you, son, whether you really are my son Esau or not." [22]Jacob drew near his father Isaac and he felt him and said, "The voice is Jacob's voice, but the hands are Esau's hands." [23]He did not recognize him because his hands were hairy like his brother Esau's hands, and he blessed him.

[24]So he said, "Are you really my son Esau?" and he said, "I am." [25]He said, "Bring it near so I can eat some of my son's game, so I can give you my personal blessing." He took it near him and he ate, and he brought him wine and he drank. [26]His father Isaac said to him, "Do draw near and kiss me, son." [27]He drew near and kissed him, and he smelled his clothes. So he blessed him, saying, "See, my son's smell is like the smell of the countryside that Yahweh has blessed. [28]God give you from the dew of the heavens and from the richness of the earth, much grain and new wine. [29]Peoples are to serve you, nations to bow down to you. Be lord to your brothers; your mother's sons are to bow down to you. Cursed be the people who curse you, blessed be those who bless you."

[30]Just as Isaac had finished blessing Jacob and Jacob had gone out from his father Isaac's presence, his brother Esau came in from his hunting. [31]He, too, made a dish and brought it to his father and said to his father, "May my father get up and eat some of his son's game, so that you may give me your personal blessing." [32]His father Isaac said to him, "Who are you?" He said, "I'm your son, your firstborn, Esau." [33]Isaac trembled, trembled with force, and said, "Then who was it that hunted game and brought it to me and I ate of it all before you came and blessed him? Yes, he will come to be blessed."

It's amazing how foolish we can be as parents. A little while ago my wife and I were having dinner with some friends, and I made some remark about how people are always talking about intimacy and the importance of being relational but that it's all talk; they all then go back to living in their single apartments. A therapist friend protested, with some anguish arising from her experience with her clients: "But they are disabled for intimacy." That phrase has stayed with me. What had disabled them? They had never known two parents relating in intimate and committed fashion to one another nor relating in intimate fashion to their children. Even the parents who stayed together (but consider the divorce rate) never had real time for their children because they were so focused on their work—paradoxically, in part because they wanted to be able to provide for their children in the present and in the future. Or maybe they were busy pressuring their children to do really well at school and be involved in lots of activities in the community in order to build up their profile when they applied to college.

We have different ways of being foolish from Isaac and Rebekah's way. Maybe as parents we don't have time or energy to favor one child over another. That was their foolishness: Isaac's favoring Esau, Rebekah's favoring Jacob. For these parents, Esau is "his son," and Jacob, "her son." It leads to deceit, blasphemy, distress, and fury.

As we come to the part of Genesis where Jacob is at the center of the story, it is even more worthwhile to imagine we are Israelites (Jacobites) listening to it. Maybe the audience shuffled their feet somewhat at the picture of Jacob grasping after Esau on his way out of Rebekah's womb—or maybe they were quite proud. Maybe they shuffled their feet somewhat at Jacob's driving a hard bargain with Esau about a helping of stew—or maybe they felt Jacob was vindicated by Esau's attaching such little value to his position as firstborn, with its privileges and responsibilities. Maybe they felt the more vindicated on hearing about Esau marrying a pair of Hittite girls, the people who lived around Hebron. The Hittites were good neighbors to Esau's grandfather, but the listeners would not be surprised that marrying local people made Isaac and Rebekah bitter. Abraham had made sure Isaac himself didn't do that, which was what had led to Rebekah's coming all the way from Aramnaharaim to marry Isaac; and Jacob will not marry a local girl.

Further, the listeners will know that no love is lost between them and the Edomites, Esau's descendants. If they live after the **exile**, these same Edomites are gradually taking over much of **Judah**'s territory, including Hebron itself.

If they do feel negative about Esau, the story puts them in their place as it unfolds. Whereas Jacob is their guy, their ancestor, he is the one who cheats Esau out of his blessing. It is hard to imagine them reckoning that the story approves of the action of Jacob the deceiver and blasphemer. God often accuses them of being deceivers, claiming to be committed to the God of Abraham but offering sacrifices to the local gods on the side to obtain their help, and claiming to trust God but hedging their bets by making astute political alliances. The religious unfaithfulness was not so clever in the end, and neither were the political alliances; they are Jacob all right, deceivers who will find that deceit does not pay.

At the same time, they will find (as happened in the relationship between Abimelech and Isaac) that God is not moralistic in making things work out. Jacob did not deserve the blessing, but God does not operate on the basis of merit. And God is quite happy to use Jacob's sinfulness in order to subvert the social order that says the first son should have the major privileges and responsibilities.

GENESIS 27:34–28:5

Words that Cannot Be Undone

³⁴When Esau heard his father's words, he cried out with a very loud and bitter cry. He said to his father, "Bless me, me as well, father!" ³⁵Isaac said, "Your brother came deceitfully and took your blessing." ³⁶He said, "He is called 'Jacob,' isn't he? He has 'grabbed' me these two times. He took my birthright, and yes, now, he has taken my blessing." So he said, "Haven't you saved a blessing for me?" ³⁷Isaac said in reply to Esau, "Actually I have made him lord in relation to you. I have given him all his brothers as servants and sustained him with grain and new wine. So what can I do for you, son?" ³⁸Esau said to his father, "Do you have one blessing, father? Bless me, me as well, father!" Esau wept aloud. ³⁹His father Isaac said in reply to him, "Yes: your

dwelling will be from the richness of the earth and from the dew of the heavens above. [40]By your sword you will live, but you will serve your brother, though as you wander you will break his yoke from your neck."

[41]Esau was hostile to Jacob because of the blessing with which his father had blessed him, and Esau said to himself, "When the days for mourning my father arrive, I shall slay my brother Jacob." [42]Rebekah was told her elder son Esau's words, and she sent and summoned her younger son Jacob, and said to him, "Well, your brother Esau is going to console himself by slaying you. [43]Now, son, listen to my voice. Take yourself off, flee to Harran to my brother Laban [44]and live with him for some time until your brother's fury goes away, [45]until your brother's anger with you goes away and he forgets what you have done to him. And I will send and get you from there. Why should I lose both of you in one day?"

[46]So Rebekah said to Isaac, "I hate my life because of the Hittite women. If Jacob gets a wife from among the Hittite women like these, from the women of this country, what good will life be for me?"

[28:1]So Isaac summoned Jacob and blessed him and charged him, "You are not to get a wife from among the Canaanite women. [2]Take yourself to Paddan-aram to the house of Bethuel, your mother's father, and get yourself a wife from there from among the daughters of Laban, your mother's brother. [3]May El Shadday bless you and make you fruitful and numerous, so that you become a community of peoples. [4]May he give to you the blessing of Abraham, to you and your offspring with you, so that you possess the country where you are residing, which God gave Abraham." [5]So Isaac sent Jacob off and he went to Paddan-aram to Laban the son of Bethuel the Aramean, the brother of Rebekah, the mother of Jacob and Esau.

In lots of ways, words are powerful things. We can say things and wish we had not said them yet be unable to get out of their implications. A woman I know stood at the front of church and made her marriage vows, then subsequently discovered that her husband had concealed from her the fact that actually he was gay and was not interested in a proper marriage relationship; he had wanted to marry to make himself respectable in the setting of a homophobic church. She so wished she had never undertaken those vows that she had made through someone's deceit, but she could not get out of them. She eventually got a divorce, but that did not exactly reinstate her as a single person in the eyes of her church or in her own eyes.

As the head of the family, Isaac has the responsibility to see things go well after his death and to see his eldest son get the resources he needs to become the new head of the family. Blessing his eldest son is the way he goes about that (there are no written wills, attorneys, laws about estate planning, or powers of attorney). His word, solemnly uttered in the context of a meal that makes it rather like a **covenant**, has that effect. So for Esau and Jacob, the implications of what happens here are critical and decisive. Esau loses his position, his responsibility, and his security. Jacob gains all those. He gains the blessing. All his life, even before he was born, he has been seeking to grab it. That is what being Jacob, grabber, means.

It makes all the difference. Except that it doesn't.

A while ago I had an e-mail from my boss about a former student who had transferred to another seminary, commenting that the student didn't seem any happier where he is now from the way he was at our seminary. I commented back that what determined whether people were happy seemed not to be (for instance) the nature of the seminary or the churches they got involved with. Happiness largely issues from inside. It is said that when people win the lottery, get married, or get a new job, for a few months this issues in greater happiness, but then they settle down to their previous level of happiness; and when people lose their jobs, their spouses, or get a chronic illness, for a few months that issues in a reasonable gloom, but then they settle back into their previous level of happiness. Later, I was myself e-mailing with that former student, and he commented on the fact that although the individual elements in his life were good, his life might have been different if he hadn't made some stupid choices. And I guess that is true, though again whether he would have been more fulfilled or more effective in serving God is a different question, given this fact that happiness largely issues from inside. Nor am I sure (I said to him) whether or not it helps us to blame ourselves—also known as "take responsibility for ourselves" (important as it is in its own right to take responsibility for ourselves).

While Esau's distraught reaction to his deception is entirely reasonable, the deception seems not to make a whole lot of difference to him and Jacob in the end. Jacob's future story will not look especially fulfilled despite gaining Isaac's blessing. He will continue to look as torn as he did on his way out of the womb. And Esau's future story will not look especially bleak. For now, he is so murderously furious that Jacob has to run for his life, but Esau will settle back into looking as casual as he did on the day he gave up his birthright for some lentil stew and will welcome Jacob back with open arms.

Meanwhile the fracas provides a reason for Rebekah to maneuver Isaac to send Jacob off to do what Abraham's servant had done for Isaac in getting him a wife from "back east." That assures the audience that for all his faults there was no dubious intermarrying between Jacob and the local women. For those later generations, it was an important principle because of the ease with which such involvement with the local peoples in their day led Jacob's descendants astray in their commitment to God. Once again, in other words, the covert question here concerns not whether it is OK to marry across ethnic lines but whether it is OK to marry across religious lines.

The four complementary ways these chapters speak about God are instructive. They recur in Genesis (see the comments on Genesis 17:1–6): (1) In his opening conversation with Esau about the blessing, Isaac speaks of God as **Yahweh**, the one who will be revealed to Moses and thus to Israel as involved with them and active in their midst; this same God was active in the ancestors' day. (2) Isaac prays that **El Shadday** will give the blessing of Abraham to Isaac. In general terms, Israel's ancestors shared this way of speaking about God with the local peoples, so that Melchizedek could speak of God as El Elyon, "God Most High." Such expressions complement the distinctive Israelite name "Yahweh" by presupposing an overlap between what other peoples know about God and what Israel knows. (3) In addressing his father, Jacob himself speaks of "your God," and God earlier appeared to Isaac with the introduction "I am the God of your father Abraham" (Genesis 26:24). This kind of expression draws attention to God's distinctive involvement with Israel's ancestors in guiding this family. God is not settled in a place, because this people is not settled in a place, but God has a settled involvement with this family whereby God leads and guides their head, to keep them on track toward fulfillment of the intention to bless the world through them. God is God of Abraham, then of Isaac; when Jacob is head of the family, God will be God of Jacob. (4) God is—well, God. Simply God. The only one.

GENESIS 28:6–15

The Stairway to Heaven

⁶Esau saw that his father Isaac had blessed Jacob and sent him off to Paddan-aram to get himself a wife from there, and in blessing him had charged him, saying, "You are not to get a wife from among the Canaanite women," ⁷and Jacob had obeyed his father and mother and gone to Paddan-aram. ⁸So Esau saw that his father Isaac did not like the Canaanite women. ⁹Esau went to Ishmael and got as wife Mahalath the daughter of Ishmael, Abraham's son, sister of Nebaioth, in addition to the wives he had.

¹⁰Jacob left Beersheba and went to Harran. ¹¹He reached a place and spent the night there because the sun had set. He took one of the stones from the place and put it at his head and lay down in that place. ¹²And he had a dream. There—a ramp was set up on the ground with its top reaching to the heavens. There—God's aides were going up and down on it. ¹³And there—Yahweh was standing by him. He said, "I am Yahweh, the God of your father Abraham and the God of Isaac. The ground that you are lying on, I will give to you and to your offspring. ¹⁴Your offspring will be like the earth's dust. You will spread out west, east, north, and south. All the families of the earth will bless themselves by you and your offspring. ¹⁵Yes: I will be with you. I will keep you wherever you go and bring you back to this country, because I will not leave you until I have done what I have told you."

When I would occasionally remember a dream and report it, my wife would say that she didn't dream. Really she knew she did, because everyone does; it's one reason why we sleep. But

we don't usually remember our dreams, maybe partly because
they are part of our processing things. Now, as I get older, I
don't sleep as well as I did when I was younger, but because I
sometimes wake up during the night, I remember my dreams,
which can be disturbing but is often fun. A few nights ago, I
dreamed that one of our church-history professors was playing for the Welsh soccer team and scored a magnificent goal.
I don't know what that was about. Last night I dreamed I had
three books on the subject of Wisdom in the Old Testament to
review for journals and that the reviews were almost due, so I
was pleased to wake up and remember that I had only one book
on Psalms to review, though I also have quite a few student
papers on Wisdom to grade. In our dreams we are indeed often
processing questions, problems, and upcoming tasks.

No doubt Jacob is doing this. He is on his way out of Canaan,
on his way out of the promised land. He has started from the
effective southern boundary of the country at Beersheba and
still has a long road ahead of him to get to Dan, the northern boundary, and then a longer road beyond that to get to
Paddan-aram. He has never been even as far as Bethel before,
and mentally he is out of the country already. It is not surprising that he has some processing to do.

We will discover in a moment that he is actually in the
center of the country, close to a place where his grandfather
once pitched his tents, built an **altar**, and prayed when he first
arrived (Genesis 12:6–8). It might even be the same place,
though Genesis does not say so, and if it was, apparently Jacob
does not realize it. But Genesis keeps repeating the word for
"place," which often refers to a shrine or sanctuary, a sacred
place (as, indeed, in Genesis 12:6). Certainly this ended up as
a sacred place.

His dream is not merely a matter of subjective processing.
In the Bible, dreams are often a way God speaks to people,
sometimes in relation to issues that they are needing to process, though sometimes not. Jacob sees a ramp or a staircase
joining the heavens and the earth. We don't know exactly how
to translate the word and thus exactly how to picture it (the
word comes only here, but it looks as if it refers to something
that "goes up," and it is related to words that mean a highway).

Evidently it constitutes a link between the heavens and the earth, a way for God's **aides** to move between the two (remember, angels don't have wings; they walk).

What God does in Jacob's dream is open his eyes to something that is happening all the time; the scene parallels one where Elisha prays for his servant to be able to see the supernatural forces that protect them when they are in danger (2 Kings 6). It is continually the case that God is involved in the world and sending aides on missions. You cannot see them, but they are at work. Jacob has every reason to be apprehensive about his situation. He has lied to his father, taken God's name in vain, cheated his father, made Esau want to kill him, and had to set out on his way out of the promised land. God steps in to give him reassurance that all this does not mean God's purpose will be frustrated. God's aides are still at work not because Jacob deserves to have God active in his life but because God will not be put off from acting just by Rebekah and Jacob's stupidity. Not only does God enable him to see the aides who are continually active in God's work in the world, but God personally shows up in the dream, without electrocuting Jacob, to give him a special message of encouragement.

God begins with another phrase that comes here for the first time but will often recur in the Old Testament: "I am **Yahweh**." It is a kind of self-announcement. Now, when I say, "I am John Goldingay," I am introducing myself to someone I have not met before. On the other hand, when the U.S. president introduces a speech by saying, "I am the president of the United States," it does not mean "You don't know who I am, so here is the information about that." It means "I remind you who I am, because it is the basis for what I am about to say when I declare my intentions or make promises." So it is when God speaks to Jacob. All the power and authority of Yahweh lie behind the promises that will follow.

There is a kind of shorthand involved in that phrase "I am Yahweh." Israelites know that Yahweh is the only God. So in a way, saying, "I am Yahweh" is like saying, "I am God." Yet it says more, because it reminds people who hear this self-announcement that their own God simply is God. It is as if the U.S. president introduces himself with his name, saying, "I am

John F. Kennedy, and . . ." or "I am Barack Obama and. . . ." All the power and authority of the president are embodied in this person. All the power and authority of God are represented in Yahweh. Adding, "the God of your father Abraham and the God of Isaac" underlines the point. Historically, that is more likely what God would have said to Jacob (given that the actual name "Yahweh" was first revealed to Moses). And this further description is one that would bring home to Jacob again the power and authority of the God who has been involved with his grandfather and his father, making promises to them and showing faithfulness in taking them toward the fulfillment of those promises.

That leads directly into the commitments God goes on to make to Jacob. In a way all God says is, "You know those promises to Abraham and Isaac? They apply to you, too, even though at this moment you are fleeing the country. They mean I will be with you on this journey that is both shameful (because you are on the run) and auspicious (because you are going to find a wife from your own people)." The promise to be with Jacob takes up the promise to Isaac when he was under pressure (Genesis 26:1–5) and again implies that God will be with Jacob not merely in such a way as to make him *feel* okay but also in a way that ensures he *is* okay, kept safe in that foreign country until he is able to return.

GENESIS 28:16–29:14a

How to Live in a Contractual Relationship with God

[16]Jacob awoke from his sleep and said, "Yahweh is definitely here in this place, and I myself didn't know!" [17]He was in awe, and he said, "How awesome is this place! This is none other than 'God's house'! This is the gate of the heavens!" [18]Early in the morning Jacob took the stone where he had set his head and set it up as a pillar and poured oil on the top of it. [19]He named the place Beth-el (Luz was the name of the city previously, however). [20]And Jacob made a vow, saying, "If God will be with me, and keeps me on this journey that I am going on, and gives me food to eat and clothes to wear, [21]and I come back in peace to my father's house, then Yahweh will be God for me,

²²and this stone that I have set up as a pillar will be God's house, and everything that you give me I will rigorously tithe to you." ²⁹:¹Jacob got going and went to the country of the Easterners. ²He looked, and there—a well in the open country, and three flocks of sheep lying there by it, because people watered the flocks from that well. The stone on the well's mouth was big. ³All the flocks would gather there, and they would roll the stone off the well's mouth and water the sheep, and put the stone back in its place on the well's mouth. ⁴Jacob said to them, "Brothers, where are you from?" They said, "We're from Harran." ⁵He said to them, "Do you know Laban, the son of Nahor?" They said, "We do." ⁶He said to them, "Is he well?" They said, "He's well. There—his daughter Rachel is coming with the flock." ⁷He said, "Now. It's still the middle of the day. It's not time for the livestock to be gathered. Water the sheep and go and pasture them." ⁸They said, "We can't, until all the flocks are gathered and the stone is rolled from on the well's mouth and we have watered the sheep." ⁹While he was still speaking with them, Rachel came with the sheep belonging to her father, because she was a shepherd. ¹⁰When Jacob saw Rachel, the daughter of Laban, his mother's brother, and the sheep of Laban, his mother's brother, Jacob went up and rolled the stone from on the well's mouth and watered the sheep of Laban his mother's brother; ¹¹and Jacob kissed Rachel and wept aloud. ¹²Jacob told Rachel that he was a relative of her father and that he was Rebekah's son, and she ran and told her father. ¹³When Laban heard the news of his sister's son, Jacob, he ran to meet him, hugged him and kissed him, and brought him into his house. He told Laban all that had happened, ¹⁴ᵃand Laban said to him, "Yes, you are my own flesh and blood."

I was trying to explain to a group of Christians the difference between a **covenant** and a contract in order to suggest that God's relationship with us is more like the former than the latter. I have a contract with the phone company and with the publishers of this book. I pay my phone bill; the phone company makes my phone work. I produce a manuscript; the publisher pays me a royalty. No payment; no phone connection; no phone connection; no payment. No manuscript; I have to return the advance. But I have a covenantal relationship with my wife. I am committed to her no matter what happens, whether or not she can "deliver" what one might expect from a wife. When you marry someone, you don't say, "I will commit myself to you on condition that you commit yourself to me." "Oh yes you do," said one of the people in the group. I was a bit thrown by that—so thrown that I didn't ask whether he was married. All I could say was that I thought he had an odd idea of marriage. Of course marriage is a two-sided **commitment**, but it seems to me that describing it in terms of contract and conditions obscures the nature of the relationship.

I suspect Jacob also had a contractual understanding of his relationship with God. It would not be surprising, because that is the way Jacob operates in other relationships. His initial response to his dream seems powerful and profound. The place where he has the dream is "House-of-God," Beth-el. We know about Bethel from the accounts of Abraham's experiences. Maybe Genesis 12–13 was using the name there because it would be the name the people listening to the story would know (though at the time it would have been known as Luz). Or maybe God's-House was already the name of a sanctuary near Luz, and (as happens with other names) Jacob is seeing a new significance in it. If Jacob was thinking of a new name, then one would have thought he would have called it "God's Gate" or "God's Stairway" rather than "God's House." For those people hearing the story, it would suggest something else. After Israel split into two nations after David and Solomon's day, Bethel and Dan were the two places where **Ephraim** set up its main sanctuaries to replace Jerusalem, so this story would either provide some basis for valuing Bethel as a place where God appeared or show how a place where God had appeared can be somewhere that gets misused—according to which side you were on.

It is Jacob's subsequent reflections that raise the question about how he understood his relationship with God. First, there is the series of "if" clauses. There are no "if" clauses in God's words to Jacob (no clauses such as "if you obey me" or "if you start telling the truth" or "if you give up your obsession with the blessing"). It is just as well. While God can go in for "if" clauses, God is not usually so lucky as to have people fulfill them. God's words to Cain in Genesis 4:7 are the nearest God comes to one in Genesis. If God waited for there to be people who would fulfill "if" clauses before working through them, God would wait forever. In contrast, Jacob turns God's simple promises into a whole sequence of "if" clauses, then adds, "Okay, if Yahweh will do all that, Yahweh can be my God." The irony is underlined by the undertaking that follows: "You give me all that, and I'll give a tenth back to you." That's fair, isn't it? There is nothing contractual about the relationship God wants to have with Jacob, but there is everything contractual about the relationship Jacob wants to have with God. Jacob is always the calculator.

Once again, this would set the audience thinking. Later, God will indeed say, "If you really obey my voice and keep my covenant, you will be my treasure among all the peoples" (Exodus 19:5); it is the next "if" clause after Genesis 4:7. By then, God has already kept the promise to turn Abraham and Sarah's offspring into a great nation and to bring them out of Egypt, so God now feels free to utter an "if." But that runs the risk of giving the impression that the relationship is contractual. We human beings may like that; it gives us a sense of control. There is a list of rules to fulfill, and we can fulfill them and then "know" God will be pleased with us. But that does not really work in personal relationships, and it does not work in a relationship with God. When the people who call themselves "Jacob-Israel" read this story, they are invited to recognize this instinct in themselves and to note the difference between God's way of looking at the relationship and Jacob's.

When he gets to Paddan-aram, Jacob finds himself again the beneficiary of grace, though he then finds that a contract again suits him, as it suits his prospective father-in-law.

GENESIS 29:14b–31

The Deceiver Deceived

[14b]He stayed with him for a full month. [15]Then Laban said to Jacob, "Are you a relative of mine, but are you to work for me for nothing? Tell me what your wages should be." [16]Now Laban had two daughters. The elder was called Leah and the younger

was called Rachel. [17]Leah's eyes were soft, but Rachel had a lovely figure and a lovely face, [18]and Jacob loved Rachel. So he said, "I will work for you for seven years for your younger daughter, Rachel." [19]Laban said, "Giving her to you will be better than giving her to another man. Stay with me." [20]So Jacob served seven years for Rachel, but they seemed like a few days because of his love for her. [21]Then Jacob said to Laban, "Give me my wife, since my time is completed, so that I may sleep with her." [22]So Laban gathered all the people of the place and made a feast, [23]but in the evening he took his daughter Leah and brought her to him, and he slept with her. ([24]Laban gave his maidservant Zilpah to his daughter Leah as her maidservant.)

[25]So in the morning: There, it was Leah! Jacob said to Laban, "What is this that you have done to me? Was it not for Rachel that I served with you? Why have you deceived me?" [26]Laban said, "It is not done like that among us, giving the younger before the elder. [27]Complete the week for this one, and I will give you that one as well, in return for serving with me for another seven years more." [28]Jacob did so. He completed the week for one, and he gave him his daughter Rachel as wife. ([29]Laban gave his maidservant Bilhah to his daughter Rachel as her maidservant.) [30]So Jacob also slept with Rachel, and indeed loved Rachel more than Leah, and served with him another seven years more. [31]But Yahweh saw that Leah was unloved and opened her womb, whereas Rachel was infertile.

The chapters in *Genesis for Everyone* regularly begin with a story making a link with our own world, but who needs a story to introduce the account of Jacob's wedding? If I made a list of the moments in the Bible that I would most like to have witnessed (at least, a slightly frivolous list), then at the top would be seeing the look on Jacob's face the morning after. The way Genesis tells the story invites you to imagine the scene: in the dark of evening Jacob could not see who was coming to him, but when morning dawns, "There, it was Leah!" The person he has married is not the person he thought it was (of course, all married couples have that experience one way or another). The great deceiver has become the one deceived. The younger cannot have priority over the elder: that was just the principle Jacob had defied, in his deceit of Isaac. Poor Jacob has lived by the principle that "true love waits," and he wants to be able to give expression to all the libido he has been storing up for seven years. But in Laban, Jacob has met his match. He expresses his libido all right, but not in the direction he had in mind. So he completes the honeymoon week with Leah and then starts again with Rachel and knuckles down for another seven years of work for Laban.

Like most societies, Middle Eastern culture assumes there are some economic arrangements associated with marriage, one of whose major significances is to seal good relationships between families and provide a framework for handling the consequences of the marriage breaking down or one of the partners dying (in the modern West, we have showers, bridal registers, receptions, prenuptial agreements, and laws about maintenance and about the rights of surviving partners). These include the giving of substantial gifts. These gifts would some-times come from the bride's family to the groom's family; the dowry the maidservants Leah and Rachel bring would be part of that, and they illustrate how this dowry remains something that belongs to the bride, though the groom may benefit from it. Sometimes they come from the groom's family to the bride's (to talk about a "bride price" is misleading, because there is no more assumption that the groom comes to own his wife than there is when a Western marriage service involves a father passing on his daughter to the groom). "Bride service," another expression of this principle, involves the groom working for the bride's family; that is the pattern here.

Jacob is doing what Genesis 2 literally says; he has left his father and mother and is uniting with his wife in the context of her family (usually in Israel a girl would join her husband in the context of his family). If seven years seems a long time to wait, we may need to bear in mind that Rachel would likely be just a young teenager and perhaps not actually ready for mar-riage when Jacob and Laban undertake their negotiation.

The rest of the story accepts in matter-of-fact fashion the way family life could work in that cultural context, with over-laps and contrasts with the way things can turn out in any mod-ern cultural context. Like Abraham and Sarah, and presumably Isaac and Rebekah, Laban has a household that is an extensive family business. He is a major sheep farmer with a household big enough to support maidservants that he can pass on to his two daughters when they marry. They will then help their mistresses run their own households in semi-independence from those of their father. There are patriarchal assumptions written into the way things work. A woman's self-esteem and significance are tied to her capacity to have children, so not being able to do so is a monumental deprivation.

In all of this, God is involved. Rachel has the love, so God sees to it that Leah has the babies. There is a significant disjunction between the way Genesis comments on Rachel's infertility and Leah's fertility. It is God who makes Leah fertile, but it is not God who makes Rachel infertile. In some sense, of course, God is responsible for both; but there is a positive intentionality about the way God gets involved with Leah in her sadness. Genesis speaks of God's closing wombs (see Genesis 20:18), but God is more likely to pay personal attention to opening wombs. You cannot say this is always how things work out. Sometimes the beautiful, clever woman who is married to a man who dotes on her is also the woman who gets the baby (I know, because I was that husband). Sometimes the ordinary girl for whom marriage and motherhood would mean fulfillment is the woman who cannot get pregnant. But sometimes God acts to make things work out in a way that redresses imbalances.

Once again, God is involved in all of this. You could even wonder it if might have been God's plan. After all, God is committed to making the offspring of Abraham and of Isaac and of Jacob into a numerous people. At some point someone is going to need to produce a lot of children. These two women and their two maidservants are going to produce the ancestors of Israel's twelve clans (we usually call them tribes, but as they belong to the same people, clans is a better word). As the Israelite people listened to these stories in the family or the village or at great festivals and heard about Leah, Rachel, Zilpah, and Bilhah, and in due course about Reuben, Simeon, Levi, and so on, they were hearing about their own origins and sometimes learning about factors lying behind their relationships with one another.

GENESIS 29:32–30:3

I Want to Know What Love Is

³²So Leah became pregnant and bore a son, and called him Reuben, because (she said), "Yahweh has 'seen' my ill treatment, because now my husband will 'love me.'" ³³She became pregnant again and bore a son, and said, "Yahweh has 'heard' that I am unloved and has given me this one as well," so she called him Simeon. ³⁴She became pregnant again and bore a son, and said, "Now this time my husband will become 'attached' to me, because I have born him three sons." Hence he was called Levi. ³⁵She became pregnant again and bore a son and said, "This time I will 'confess' Yahweh." Hence she called him Judah. Then she stopped having children.

³⁰:¹Rachel saw that she did not give birth for Jacob, and Rachel was jealous of her sister and said to Jacob, "Give me children! Otherwise, I am going to die!" ²Jacob was furious with Rachel, and said, "Am I in place of God, who has withheld from you the fruit of the womb?" ³She said, "Here is my maidservant Bilhah. Sleep with her, so that she can give birth on my knees and I can be built up as well through her."

I have just read a review of a TV program about polygamy in the United States. It incidentally notes how one motivation for polygamy is that it can be a route to more children and more money, which fits with the assumptions about polygamy in the Old Testament (the Old Testament adds that multiplying wives is a sign of status). The review also includes the following comment: "In spite of its seeming celebration of diverse family arrangements, the show bristles with so much pain that nearly every character seems marked for spiritual death, the way characters on 'The Sopranos' used to be marked for actual death." We are inclined to assume that marriage has something to do with love, and we may then have a hard time understanding polygamy. (People in other cultures may assume marriage has something to do with commitment and may have a hard time understanding divorce.) What is the place of love and commitment in a polygamous marriage?

As is the case with Abraham and Hagar, sleeping with Bilhah (and later Zilpah) as well as Leah and Rachel does not imply Jacob is committing adultery. All four women are his wives. Genesis does not suggest polygamy is immoral, though it does recognize that its origins back in Genesis 4 were questionable; the notorious Lamech was the first polygamist. And in a story such as this one, it does show how unfortunate can be the outworkings of polygamy. Israel's experience of polygamy is comparable to much Western experience of divorce. Last Sunday's paper had a long article about the trials and tribulations of a middle-aged couple trying to unite two sets of teenagers they had brought into their marriage from previous marriages. They are succeeding, but they see a therapist twice a month, and they don't even live in California. After one session, the wife commented to the therapist, "I wish you would move in with us." It is evident from this story that Jacob's family needed a resident therapist, and it will not be surprising if relationships between all these brothers become somewhat fraught. A friend of mine who has worked in a polygamous context reported recently the comment of one of his students: that polygamy begins in lust and ends in pain. Here it begins in pain and ends in pain.

Jacob's own involvement with his women differs from that which would seem natural to most Western readers. On one hand there is his love for Rachel. When he arrived in Paddan-aram, she was the first person he met. With the bluster that is one aspect of his character (a decent deceiver needs to be a blusterer) the new guy in town set about telling the local shepherds how to do their work, and then at the sight of Rachel demonstrated that a real man has no problem rolling away a giant stone single-handedly for a pretty girl. Yet there were also lots of tears and hugs and kisses and stories to be told.

The scene reprises the one that describes how Abraham's servant found Rebekah, though it thereby draws attention to the differences from that scene. Abraham's servant is a gentleman; Jacob is a braggart. The first story kept referring to God's involvement; there is none of that in this story, though it is the process whereby the ancestors of the twelve Israelite clans will come into being. There, the servant had gone laden with the presents you need when you are looking for a wife. Here, Jacob left in circumstances that ruled that out, which might be one reason why he has to perform his seven years of service rather than seal the marriage with gifts.

In what sense did Jacob love Rachel, and why? Rachel is a very attractive girl. Is that the basis of his love? What kind of attraction did Jacob feel? Did he actually "love" her? One could as easily translate the expression by saying he "liked" her. Did he "love" Rachel more than Leah? Or did he "like" her more than Leah because she had nicer eyes and a sexy figure? Or is this one of those contexts where "love" is more an attitude of commitment than an emotion—was he more committed to Rachel than to Leah? Yet although he especially "loves" Rachel, he is quite happy to sleep with three other women.

It rather looks as if Leah, at least, assumes she is unloved in all those senses. Yet in some respects she is at the same time fooling herself or living in denial. One can see both aspects of this in the names her sons bear. Her first son is Reuben, and the first part of his name could make people think of the Hebrew word for "see," while the last part overlaps with the word for "love me." So his name can suggest God "has 'seen' my ill-treatment, because now my husband will 'love me.'" The pain in her heart is suggested by her use of the word *ill-treatment*, the word Hagar had used for her ill-treatment at the hands of Abraham and Sarah, and the word Exodus will use to describe Israel's ill-treatment in Egypt. Her second son is Simeon, whose name could make one think of the verb Hagar used when she spoke of God's heeding or hearing about her; Leah thus reflects, God "has 'heard' that I am unloved and has given me this one as well." Again, the pain in her heart is suggested by the word "unloved," which is traditionally translated "hated." It suggests not so much an emotion, or not merely that, but an attitude, a stance, and a way of acting (a "hater" is an enemy). But it does suggest that for Leah, Rachel means everything to Jacob and she means nothing. God sees that, too.

So God and Leah try again, and she gives birth to Levi, whose name could make one think of the verb for attaching oneself or joining (it is the word that comes to describe the conversion of someone to Judaism). So "now this time my husband will become 'attached' to me," she says, wrongly. Then she has her fourth son, Judah, whose name makes one think of the word meaning "thanksgiving" or "confession," and intriguingly she declares, "This time I will 'confess' Yahweh." Has she determined to praise God anyway? Or is this her last forlorn hope, that God is about to give her reason for such testimony?

GENESIS 30:4–21

The Problem of Insight

[4]So she gave him Bilhah her maidservant as wife, and Jacob slept with her. [5]Bilhah became pregnant and bore Jacob a son. [6]Rachel said, "God has 'ruled' for me. Yes, he has listened to my voice and given me a son." Hence she called him Dan. [7]Bilhah, Rachel's maidservant, became pregnant again and bore Jacob a second son. [8]Rachel said, "A supernatural 'wrestling match' I have fought with my sister. Yes, I have won." So she called him Naphtali.

[9]Leah saw that she had stopped having children and took Zilpah her maidservant and gave her to Jacob as wife. [10]Zilpah, Leah's maid, bore Jacob a son, [11]and Leah said, "'Luck' has come!" So she called him Gad. [12]Zilpah, Leah's maidservant, bore Jacob a second son, [13]and Leah said, "What 'good fortune' I have, because girls will call me 'fortunate.'" So she named him Asher.

[14]At the time of the wheat harvest, Reuben went and found love-plants in the countryside and brought them to his mother Leah. Rachel said to Leah, "Do give me some of your son's love-plants." [15]She said to her, "Was it a small thing your taking my husband, and you're also going to take my son's love-plants?" Rachel said, "So he can sleep with you tonight in return for your son's love-plants." [16]In the evening Jacob came from the wild, and Leah went out to meet him and said, "I am the one you are to sleep with, because I have paid a hire charge for you with my son's love-plants." So he slept with her that night, [17]and God gave heed to Leah. She became pregnant and bore Jacob a fifth son. [18]Leah said, "God gave me my 'hire charge,' because I gave my maidservant to my husband." So she called him Issachar. [19]Leah became pregnant again, and bore Jacob a sixth son. [20]Leah said, "God has given me a good 'endowment.' This time my husband will 'honor' me, because I have borne him six sons." So she called him Zebulun. [21]Later, she bore a daughter, and called her Dinah.

A number of my students are training to be family therapists, and they are often intrigued by these stories in Genesis. They are excited to find how dysfunctional these families are because in their own way they match our dysfunctional families, but the students are then disappointed to find how little these chapters provide by way of solutions. They do suggest moralistic solutions—don't marry more than one person; don't be jealous when someone else has a baby; don't blame your spouse for the fact that you can't have a baby (whether it is the husband or the wife who has the problem). These are good pieces of advice, though often they are useless ones. They are pretty obvious, and they would be unnecessary if we did not find it hard to heed them. It takes a degree of spiritual and emotional maturity to live by them, and most people lack that. And knowledge of how these dynamics work may not help you much. This weekend we watched a movie called *Rachel Getting Married* that has nothing to do with Rachel in Genesis but illustrates this point. Rachel is a therapist about to complete her PhD, but her "insight" about relationships within her own family only extends to her being able to put angry labels on things and use her "insight" to scorn other people. The significance of these stories in Genesis is not to provide tips on how to avoid getting into a mess or how to get out of one, but to remind us that we all get into messes and that this does not stop God from being at work.

It is easy to see this dynamic in Jacob's family. There is Leah's pain, Rachel's jealousy and anger, and Jacob's rage, and there are the strategies for coping that Rachel and Leah employ. Their story works out more like Abraham and Sarah's than Isaac and Rebekah's. I imagine Isaac and Rebekah, in better days, instinctively telling their sons stories about the events leading up to their birth (if Isaac and Rebekah were anything like my wife and me). But Jacob had apparently learned nothing from the way God was involved in the process whereby he found a wife (let alone the necessity to take your marriage gifts with you to avoid having to work for seven years in connection with acquiring the woman you love), and nothing about what to do when your wife can't get pregnant (Isaac prayed). God did come into the conversation about that, but only in a rhetorical way. Jacob talked to Rachel *about* God, but he didn't talk *to*

God. Similarly, Rachel had tackled Jacob in connection with her inability to get pregnant rather than following the example of her aunt Rebekah, who had tackled God about the problems in her pregnancy, and Rachel followed the example of her great-aunt Sarah in the way she proposed they deal with the problem. Like Hagar, Bilhah was a kind of surrogate for Rachel (she would literally have her baby while lying between Rachel's legs so that it is as if Rachel has the baby). To us this may seem tough for Bilhah, though for her it may have been OK. She got the status of a wife, even if a secondary wife, and even if in one sense her children would count as Rachel's, everyone would always know she was the one who bore them. Certainly the result was less unhappy than was the case with Abraham, Sarah, Hagar, and Ishmael.

As with Leah's children, their significance is written into Rachel's comments on "her" children's names (Genesis itself describes them as children Bilhah bears for Jacob). The first is Dan, whose name will always remind her that God "ruled" or made a decision for her. God had heard her voice, she adds. Had she prayed after all, then, like Aunt Rebekah? Or had God simply heard her laying into Jacob? It would not be the only occasion when God hears someone when he or she is not praying and responds. God did that for her uncle Ishmael (Genesis 21:17) and will do it for her descendants in Egypt (Exodus 2:23–25). The second child is Naphtali, whose name will always remind her of how she "wrestled" with Leah for Jacob's love. It was (literally) "wrestlings of God" she engaged in, "divine wrestlings," "supernatural wrestlings." Like Jacob, she is using God's name only rhetorically, as we might say, "It was a divine evening." This was a really serious war between the two wives. Rachel was in danger of losing because she had the love but not the children; but eventually she has both, so she has won.

Leah doesn't give up. Being now unable to get pregnant, she gets Jacob also to marry her maidservant Zilpah. (What does Jacob think of all this? There is no doubt that the wives in these stories are capable of exercising headship over their husbands!). Both Zilpah's son's names, Gad and Asher, would make one think of "good luck" or "good fortune." In turn, Rachel doesn't give up. The word for "love-plants" is usually translated "mandrakes," but it looks like a word linked to love (we don't know if they did correspond to what is known as mandrakes, but mandrakes have an overlapping reputation). The implication is either that they arouse sexual feelings or that they (thereby?) encourage fertility. Strikingly, Genesis declares not that the love-plants worked but that "God paid heed to Leah." Maybe God used the love-plants, or maybe God just did what God wanted to do, despite the love-plants and despite the sex-for-hire element in the story. Once more, God shrugs shoulders and works through or despite our human strangeness. So Leah has a son whose name will be neatly reminiscent of the process whereby she conceived him. Then she has another son whose name will both remind her of the wonder of her endowment and give her opportunity to indicate that she still longs to come first for her husband; evidently she knows she does not. Then she has a daughter. Statistically it is presumably unlikely that all these women have borne only sons over the past decade or so; indeed, Genesis will later refer to Jacob's daughters. Dinah is mentioned because she will have an important if rather unfortunate role to play in a few chapters' time. Omitting to tell us more about Jacob's other daughters does not mean that the women do not count at all, and we have seen that the women Genesis portrays (Sarah, Hagar, Rebekah, and now Jacob's four wives) are not people you could mess with. But in a patriarchal society the men exercise the formal authority, even if the women also exercise practical power and show themselves as strong as the men. And it will be Jacob's twelve *sons* who give their names to the twelve Israelite clans.

GENESIS 30:22–43

The Competition to Be the Shrewdest Sheep Farmer

[22]But God was mindful of Rachel. God paid heed to her and opened her womb, [23]and she became pregnant and bore a son, and said, "God has 'taken away' my disgrace." [24]So she called him Joseph, saying, "May Yahweh 'add' another son to me!" [25]When Rachel had born Joseph, Jacob said to Laban, "Send me off so that I may go to my homeland. [26]Give me my wives and my children for whom I have served you, so that I may go,

because you acknowledge the service I have given you." [27]Laban said to him, "If I have found favor in your eyes, I have divined that Yahweh has blessed me because of you." [28]So he said, "Specify your wages to me and I will give it to you." [29]He said to him, "You yourself acknowledge how I have served you and how your livestock have been with me, [30]because the little that you had before I came has flourished greatly. Yahweh has blessed you wherever I have been. But now, when am I myself also to do something for my own household?" [31]He said, "What shall I give you?" Jacob said, "Do not give me anything. If you will do this thing for me, I will again pasture your flocks, I will keep them. [32]I will go through all your flocks today, removing from there every speckled and spotted sheep and every dark sheep among the lambs and the spotted and speckled among the goats. It will be my wages. [33]My faithfulness will testify for me on the future day when you come to look at my wages with you. Every one with me that is not speckled or spotted among the goats or dark among the lambs: that one will have been stolen." [34]Laban said, "Right, yes, let it be as you say." [35]But that day he removed the streaked and spotted he-goats and all the speckled and spotted she-goats, every one that had white on it, and every dark one among the lambs, and put them in the care of his sons. [36]He put three days' journey between him and Jacob while Jacob was pasturing the rest of Laban's flocks.

[37]Jacob got for himself fresh rods of poplar, and almond and plane tree, and peeled white stripes in them by exposing the white that was on the rods. [38]The rods that he had peeled he stationed in the troughs, the water containers that the flocks came to drink from, in front of the flocks. When they were in heat and came to drink, [39]the flocks were in heat by the rods, and the flocks bore streaked, speckled, and spotted young. [40]The lambs Jacob set apart, and put the faces of the flocks towards the streaked and the completely dark animals in Laban's flock. So he put herds for himself separately and did not put them with Laban's flock. [41]When the strong females were in heat, Jacob would put the rods in the troughs before the eyes of the flocks so they were in heat by the rods. [42]But with the feebler in the flocks, he did not put them there. So the feeble ones were Laban's and the strong ones were Jacob's. [43]And the man became very, very prosperous. He had large flocks, female and male servants, camels, and donkeys.

After church this morning, one of our senior laypeople asked me about Hagar. Someone had implied in a comment to her that Hagar was a prostitute and/or a concubine. In effect I explained that Hagar's status was more like that of Bilhah and Zilpah, who were "legal" wives of Jacob, though they had a secondary status. We went on to discuss the rights and wrongs of the way Abraham treated Hagar, and the woman I was talking with commented, "And Abraham is our father! He wasn't much of a father!" "Too right," I said, and compared him with David. The preacher had talked about David in his sermon, and about the way during his life he himself had to face questions about destructive aspects of his lifestyle and be willing to give them up. Abraham, David: they were heroes of faith but also people with clay feet. This is such an encouragement because we are people with clay feet.

Jacob was certainly such a man, with clay hands, heart, and mind. He continues to be the great deceiver and in this story continues taking part with Laban in the network TV contest for the "Deceiver of the Year" award. But first, after all those years of wishing, hoping, and envying, Rachel has a son of her own. Joseph's name looks rather like the word for "take away," and it is exactly the same as the word for "may he add," which flags for us the fact that she has not finished having children yet, now that she has at last started. It is slightly odd that Genesis makes no mention of how Joseph will end up in authority over all the brothers and that the Joseph clan will be so big it splits into two clans that will carry the names of Joseph's own sons, **Ephraim** and Manasseh. The two clans will so dominate northern Israel that the first of these names will become a standard way of referring to the northern Israelite state; and from her grave Rachel will be satisfied.

Meanwhile, Jacob decides it is time to get back to **Canaan**. He has more than served his fourteen years for Leah and Rachel. Laban has a telling reason for not wanting him to leave: Laban is a very successful sheep farmer, and he knows it is because of Jacob. The way he expresses this awareness gives an example of the ongoing mixture in these stories of traditional religion and the special nature of God's involvement with these families. It is through divination that Laban knows Jacob is the secret of his success. Divination involves looking for some sign (for instance, in nature) that may give the answer to a question. A traditional British way of doing so involves looking for patterns in the tea leaves left in a cup after drinking the tea, and Genesis 44:5 will later refer to divination involving a cup. But Genesis 31 will refer to Laban's **effigies**, which were likely related to divination. The Old Testament will later disapprove of divination because it is often associated with other religions and it ignores the ways of finding guidance that God has given Israel. But here Laban testifies that what he learned by divination was that **Yahweh** had blessed him because of Jacob. He uses the special name of Israel's God and testifies to the fulfillment of Yahweh's own promise to bring blessing to the world through Abraham, Isaac, and Jacob. God had reaffirmed that promise to Jacob himself as he was on his way out of Canaan and on his way to Paddan-aram (Genesis 28:14). Laban unwittingly testifies to its fulfillment.

There is no indication that Jacob said, "Oh, wow!" and bowed down to worship God, as Abraham's servant would have done in Genesis 24, but that doesn't matter too much. We as readers know that this is what is going on. Jacob's concern is to get out of here, which is itself quite appropriate. That same purpose of God's gives Jacob a job to do back in Canaan, the country that is the base for the fulfillment of God's promises. He has obligations to his own household. He proposes a reasonable deal. He will stay a little longer. Then, despite the extent of the prosperity he has brought Laban, he will take home just the relatively small number of sheep that are not white and of goats that are not dark. It will be easy to tell if he has been honest. Laban wisely agrees, but then removes such sheep and goats as are among the flock at present so that the chance is very low that the flock Jacob now pastures will give birth to many offspring of this kind. But Jacob the expert sheep breeder knows how to defeat that plan, which apparently involves the sheep-and-goat equivalent to love-plants. If you are confused by the details of how Jacob makes this work, join the club. For me, it is a bit like understanding the internal combustion engine; for five minutes I have got it, but after that, it has gone again. Yet the result is clear. This time the shrewd Laban has met his match in the even cleverer Jacob.

GENESIS 31:1–29

The Divisiveness of Stuff

[1]He heard things that Laban's sons were saying: "Jacob has taken everything that was our father's. From what was our father's he has made all this wealth." [2]And Jacob saw Laban's attitude to him: It was not as it had been in previous days. [3]Yahweh said to Jacob, "Go back to your ancestors' country, your homeland, and I will be with you."

[4]Jacob sent and called for Leah and Rachel to come to the open country, to his flocks, [5]and said to them, "I see that your father's attitude to me is not as it was in previous days. But my father's God has been with me. [6]You know that I have served your father with all my energy, [7]and your father—he has mocked me and changed my wages ten times. But God did not let him do me harm. [8]If he would say, 'The speckled will be your wages,' all the flock would bear speckled young. If he would say, 'The streaked will be your wages,' all the flock would bear streaked young. [9]God took away your father's livestock and gave them to me. [10]At the time of the flock's mating, in a dream I looked and saw: There, the rams that were mounting the flock were streaked, speckled, and mottled. [11]In the dream God's aide said to me, 'Jacob!' I said, 'I'm here!' [12]He said, 'Now. Look up, and see. All the rams that are mounting the flock are streaked, speckled, and mottled, because I have seen everything that Laban has been doing to you. [13]I am the God of Bethel, where you anointed a pillar, where you made a vow to me. Now. Up, get out of this country and go back to your homeland.'" [14]Rachel and Leah answered by saying to him, "Do we still have a share, an inheritance, in our father's house? [15]We count as outsiders to him, because he sold us and also totally consumed the money paid for us. [16]Because all the wealth that God has taken away from our father: it belongs to us and our children. So now, do everything that God has said to you."

[17]So Jacob set off. He put his children and wives on camels [18]and drove all the livestock and all the wealth that he had acquired, the livestock he possessed that he had gained in Paddan-aram, to go to his father Isaac in the country of Canaan; [19]Laban had gone to shear his flocks. Rachel stole the effigies that belonged to her father [20]and Jacob stole away without Laban the Aramean knowing, by not telling him that he was

fleeing ²¹when he fled with all that he had. So he set off and crossed the River and headed for the mountains of Gilead.

²²Laban was told on the third day that Jacob had fled. ²³He took his brothers with him and chased after him seven days' journey, and reached him in the mountains of Gilead. ²⁴But God came to Laban the Aramean in a dream by night and said to him, "Be careful not to say anything to Jacob, good or harm."

²⁵So Laban reached Jacob when Jacob had pitched his tents in the mountains and Laban had camped with his brothers in the mountains of Gilead. ²⁶Laban said to Jacob, "What have you done? You stole away without me knowing and you drove my daughters like captives of the sword. ²⁷Why did you hide your flight and steal away from me and not tell me? I would have sent you off with rejoicing and singing, with timbrel and lyre. ²⁸You did not let me kiss my sons and daughters. Now you have been foolish in doing that. ²⁹I have it in my power to do you harm. But the God of your fathers said to me last night, 'Be careful not to say anything to Jacob, good or bad.'

Money divides people from one another. A news item this week related how a twenty-five-year feud had been simmering in a particular family. When the father died, with the mother's collusion his son concealed his father's ownership of a number of properties and the existence of a will dividing his estate among the son and his two sisters. It was, said the news, "a betrayal of biblical proportions." After five years, the two daughters discovered the deception, and they fought for twenty-five years to acquire their share of the estate. In an affidavit, one of them said, "The conspiracy to deny us our inheritance destroyed my family, broke my heart and left me with scars that I have painfully struggled with and have not fully overcome even now. . . . The deepest hurt came from my mother's role in the conspiracy. A mother is supposed to protect her child. The life my father wanted for us would have been very different."

Laban's sons are understandably resentful of the way Jacob has prospered at the expense (as they see it) of their father, and thus of themselves. Jacob himself is afraid of what Laban may do. Leah and Rachel know they have nothing to gain from Laban because Laban has nothing to gain from them now that they belong to Jacob. They also know that as long as they are with Jacob they share in all their father lost to him. Rachel steals Laban's **effigies**, and Jacob steals away from Laban. Literally Jacob steals Laban's mind, a vivid expression for keeping him in the dark about leaving and a striking expression in the context because it parallels Rachel's more literal thievery. Concern about possession and a willingness to let this concern override all considerations arising out of family relationship characterize everything that is going on.

Pasturing large flocks means spreading them out over a wide area, as is indicated by the comment in the previous chapter about Laban's moving many sheep three days' distance from Jacob. Likewise that means Jacob and his flocks are out in open country some distance away from the family base, so it is here that he has his family conference with Rachel and Leah. Thus the nature of the family business makes it easy enough for Jacob and his entourage to make a run for it without Laban's knowledge, when he is some distance away busy with sheep shearing. "The River" is the Euphrates; when Laban and his family posse catch up with Jacob, he has gone three hundred miles (in literal terms, it must have taken much more than three plus seven days) and reached Gilead, the area just east of the Jordan. He is nearly home.

Once again God is involved in all this messiness by not making a priority of seeing that people who deserve to do well prosper and that people who are not deserving fail to prosper (perhaps again because that would mean waiting forever). It is God who tells Jacob it is time to go home, though the idea has been in his head for a while. When Jacob goes on to speak of the way God has been involved with him and to relate his dream, one might wonder how far Jacob is projecting onto God his own decision making or wishful thinking. Yet Genesis confirms the basic point: God tells Jacob to go home. One would expect God eventually to do that. It is in **Canaan** that God is committed to fulfilling a purpose for the world's blessing via the blessing of Abraham's offspring. God therefore provides Jacob with another level of protection by appearing to Laban and warning him not to argue with Jacob about rights and wrongs in what has happened. Laban does not interpret this instruction too literally, but at least he does not dispute Jacob's

right to go home. His confrontation becomes one that mostly ·
concerns the way Jacob left rather than the fact that he left.

GENESIS 31:30–54

The Pain of a Family Divided by Miles

[30]Laban said, "Now. You have indeed gone because you were
very keen for your father's household. Why have you stolen my
gods?" [31]Jacob answered, saying to Laban, "Because I was
afraid, because I thought you might seize your daughters from
me. [32]The person with whom you find your gods will not
remain alive. In front of our brothers, examine for yourself
whatever I have and take it for yourself" (Jacob did not know
that Rachel had stolen them). [33] Laban went into Jacob's tent,
into Leah's tent, and into the two maidservants' tent, but did
not find them. He came out of Leah's tent and went into Rachel's
tent. [34]Now Rachel had taken the effigies, put them in the camel
saddle, and sat on them. Laban delved through everything in
the tent and did not find them. [35]She said to her father, "May
my lord not be incensed because I cannot get up before you,
because I have a period." So he searched but did not find the
effigies. [36]Jacob became incensed and argued with Laban. Jacob
testified by saying to Laban, "What is my affront, what is my
offense, that you have hunted after me? [37]When you delved
through all my possessions, what did you find of all your
household possessions? Put it here in front of my brothers and
yours so that they can give judgment between the two of us.
[38]These twenty years I have been with you. Your ewes and your
goats have not miscarried. I have not eaten rams from your
flocks. [39]I have not brought you animals that had been killed; I
myself dealt with the offense. From me you sought what was
stolen by day and what was stolen by night. [40]I became—by day
heat consumed me and by night frost. My sleep fled from my
eyes. [41]I have had these twenty years in your household; I served
you fourteen years for your two daughters and six years for
your flock, and you changed my wages ten times. [42]If the God
of my father, the God of Abraham and the Reverence of Isaac,
had not been mine, now you would have sent me off empty-
handed. But God saw my ill treatment and the toil of my hands
and gave judgment last night."

⁴³Laban testified, saying, "The daughters are my daughters, the children are my children, the flock is my flock. All that you see is mine. But what can I do today for these daughters of mine or for their children whom they have born? ⁴⁴Now, come, let's make a covenant, you and I, and it will be a witness between you and me." ⁴⁵So Jacob took a stone and set it up as a pillar. ⁴⁶Jacob said to his brothers, "Gather stones." They got stones and made a heap and ate there by the heap. ⁴⁷Laban called it Yegar-sahadutha and Jacob called it Galed. ⁴⁸Laban said, "This heap is a witness between me and you today." Hence it was called Gilead, ⁴⁹and "The Watchtower," because (he said), "Yahweh will watch between you and me when one hides from the other. ⁵⁰If you ill-treat my daughters or take wives beside my daughters, though there is no one with us, see: God will be a witness between you and me."

⁵¹And Laban said to Jacob, "Here is this heap and here is the pillar that I have set up between you and me. ⁵²This heap will be a witness and this pillar will be a witness that I am not to go past this heap to you and you are not to go past this heap to me, or this pillar, to do harm. ⁵³The God of Abraham and the God of Nahor (the God of their ancestors), decide between us." Jacob swore by the Reverence of his father Isaac. ⁵⁴Jacob made a sacrifice in the mountains and invited his relatives to eat a meal. They ate a meal and stayed the night in the mountains.

When my wife and I started dating and then wanted to get engaged, her parents were totally against it. They had some plausible reasons. I was a long-haired lout (it was the 1960s), and they weren't sure I was the kind of man they wanted to entrust their daughter to. But there was something else going on. They were very proud of their medical-student daughter, their only child, who had been the focus of their life. When she finished training, they imagined she would come back to her hometown to practice, bearing their name. Like her contemporaries, she would likely not have gone back to her hometown to practice, even if I had not come along, but they saw me as the villain who ensured it was not going to happen. What is more, I was a pastor. Fancy a doctor marrying a mere pastor! While in the long term the increasing effects of Ann's multiple sclerosis were the balm that brought healing to the relationships, in the short term it was the birth of children that led to some measure of healing. My father-in-law lived just long enough to hold both his grandsons and to watch them (or at least the older one) play with toys and play on the beach and kick a ball.

There are a few signs in this story that Jacob has some family feelings. It would be unduly cynical not to see such feelings as at least one element in his fear that Laban may take away his daughters. Jacob did, after all, love Rachel, even if he was also willing to sleep with various other women. Ironically, he is then the victim of Rachel's deception as he had been the victim of deception by her big sister and her father on his wedding night. No one can afford to trust anyone in this family. Presumably at some point he discovers that Rachel had the **effigies** all along (unless Rachel swore someone else to secrecy before her death and the information reached the author of Genesis by this other route). If Rachel had not also been so clever in concealing the effigies, it is nice to imagine the scene when Jacob discovers that the woman he loves is about to be the victim of his vow to execute the thief, a scene that will recur in the stories of Jephthah and his daughter, and Saul and his son. The author of Genesis likely sees some poetic justice in the deceiving of Laban by his own daughter, who has learned well from the characters and practice of her father and her husband (one wonders whether Laban suspected that Rachel had duped him, and even admired the way she was a true daughter of her father), as well as seeing the irony in Jacob's self-righteous and hypocritical protestations to Laban in the quasi-court case that unfolds here (the word "testify," which recurs, is a legal word).

Laban likewise evidently does have a heart beating just beneath the place where he keeps his wallet. When Jacob left, he did not take merely some sheep and goats that might or might not rightfully belong to Laban. Laban lost his daughters and his grandchildren. He has sons who can take on the family business, but they do not compensate for that loss.

There is an odd lopsidedness about the relationship of parents and their grown-up children—at least, there has been for Ann and me in relation to our parents and our grown-up children, as we have been in the one position and then in the other. It expressed itself in her parents' expectation that one day she would go "home," and it found another expression in our relationship with my parents. When we first married, they did not have a phone, and my father would go to a pay phone each Sunday just before lunchtime, push in his coins, and shout, "Are you okay?" "Yes, we're okay!" we would answer, and he would reply, "I just wanted to know that you are okay!" That would be more or less it. Later, when we lived nearer my parents and could drop by to see them more easily, I would find myself saying to Ann, "We haven't been for three or four weeks; we had better go this Sunday." Now, the shoe is on the other foot. While I am glad to get detailed news about the lives of our sons in England and their families, and we have experimented with conversations on the computer screen, I am satisfied to get a short e-mail every couple of weeks that functions mostly to reassure me that they are okay.

It was Laban who suffered through the departure of his daughters and their offspring. In travel time, they live much farther away than I live from my grandchildren. Parting with acrimony would make this much worse. It is neat, then, that despite the failure to resolve the question about the effigies the two families become reconciled and finally part happily. Laban's and Jacob's names for the place where this happens mean the same in **Aramaic** (Laban's language) and in Hebrew, with the Hebrew name also resembling the name of Gilead itself, where the meeting took place. (We will consider Jacob's distinctive title for God in connection with Genesis 32.)

GENESIS 31:55–32:24a

Fear

[55]Early in the morning Laban kissed his children and his daughters and blessed them, and Laban set off and went back to his homeland.

[32:1]As Jacob went on his way, God's aides met him. [2]When he saw them, Jacob said, "This is God's camp." He called that place Two Camps. [3]Jacob sent aides ahead of him to his brother Esau in the country of Seir, the land of Edom. [4]He instructed them, saying, "You are to say this to my lord Esau: 'Your servant

Jacob has said this: I have been staying with Laban and have remained until now. ⁵I have acquired cattle, donkeys, flocks, and male and female servants. I have sent this message to tell my lord so as to find favor in your eyes.'" ⁶The aides came back to Jacob saying, "We went to your brother Esau and yes, he is coming to meet you, and there are four hundred men with him." ⁷Jacob was very fearful. Distress came over him. He divided the people that were with him, the flocks, the cattle, and the camels, into two camps, ⁸and said, "If Esau comes to the one camp and strikes it down, the remaining camp will escape." ⁹Jacob said, "God of my father Abraham, God of my father Isaac, Yahweh, you who said to me, 'Go back to your homeland and I will be good to you,' ¹⁰I am too small for all the acts of commitment and all the steadfastness that you have shown to your servant. With my rod I crossed this Jordan and now I have become two camps. ¹¹Do save me from the hands of my brother, from the hands of Esau, because I am scared that he will come and strike me down, mothers and children. ¹²You yourself said, 'I will definitely be good to you and make your offspring like the sand of the sea, which cannot be counted because of its quantity.'"

¹³He stayed there that night and took from what he had with him a gift for his brother Esau: ¹⁴two hundred she-goats and twenty he-goats, two hundred ewes and twenty rams, ¹⁵thirty milch camels and their young, forty cows and ten bulls, and twenty she-donkeys and ten he-donkeys. ¹⁶He put them in the charge of his servants, each herd by itself, and said to his servants, "Pass on ahead of me, and keep a distance between each herd." ¹⁷He instructed the front one, "My brother Esau will meet you and ask, 'To whom do you belong? Where are you going? To whom do these belong, ahead of you?' ¹⁸You are to say, 'They are your servant Jacob's. They are a gift sent to my lord Esau. There, he himself is behind us.'" ¹⁹He also instructed both the second and the third and all the ones who followed the herds, "Speak in this way to Esau when you reach him. ²⁰And also say, 'There, your servant Jacob is behind us,'" because (he said), "If I pacify him with a gift going ahead of me and afterwards see him personally, perhaps he will accept me." ²¹So the gift passed on ahead of him, while he stayed that night in the camp. ²²That night he set off and took his two wives, his two maidservants, and his eleven children, and crossed the Jabbok

crossing. [23]So he took them and got them to cross the wash. He got what he had across the wash, [24]and Jacob was left alone.

There is something to be said for fear. On one seminary study tour to Israel and Palestine, we were on our way back from Beersheba to Jerusalem. The Israeli authorities were advising groups to follow a route that stayed in Israeli territory rather than risk trouble driving through Hebron, but that added an hour to the journey, and I knew a way of getting to Jerusalem without going through the center of Hebron. Unfortunately I got our minibuses to turn off the main road one junction too soon, and we found ourselves in another small town where people were even more hostile to Israelis. As we drove down the town's main street in our Israeli-registered vehicles, people started throwing rocks at us. I was riding shotgun, but I didn't have one, and I remember thinking, "This is a very interesting experience, though it would be as well if we got out of here." Afterward I found myself reflecting on the way other people were very scared (and incensed with me), whereas I was not. Sometimes, not being afraid is not a strength but a weakness. I don't do "scared," and I can risk things that are actually unwise. Fear is an important positive emotion. It can be debilitating, but it can keep you out of trouble.

Jacob's relationship to fear is complex. In his confrontation with Laban he used a distinctive title for God. Previously he had spoken of "the God of my father," the God who was committed to his father and made promises to his father and who he knows is also committed to him, because he stands in the line to which God has made a **commitment** in connection with fulfilling a purpose to bless his family and to bless the nations. Here he speaks of this God more specifically as the "Reverence of Isaac," the God whom Isaac reveres. It is the other side to God's being committed to him. But the Hebrew word for reverence is the same as the word for fear. There is a positive fear that expresses itself in reverence, awe, commitment, and obedience, and a negative fear that means being scared. Jacob doesn't mean Isaac is scared or frightened of God. Indeed, paradoxically, knowing a reverence and awe toward God means you increase in the confidence that can characterize your life in general.

In Jacob's case, however, it does not. Jacob is fearful of meeting Esau. He has more than one good reason. Esau is the guy who had a reason for wanting to kill him the last time they were together. And he is coming to meet Jacob with four hundred other guys. They are nearing the river Jabbok, which flows east-west from the mountains east of the Jordan and marks a point where the Jordan itself can easily be crossed and Jacob can get his company into the main part of the country.

The story underlines the irony of the situation in several ways. It rather looks as if God has guessed that Jacob will be somewhat apprehensive of meeting Esau, so God sends some **aides** to meet him. Jacob gives the name "Two Camps" to the place where this happens, and "camp" commonly denotes a military encampment, which suggests that the aides are a show of supernatural protection to encourage Jacob, like the vision of the stairway to heaven with its similarity to the vision in 2 Kings 6. One irony then lies in the way Jacob then sends off his own aides to meet Esau and divides his own "forces" into two camps, so that if Esau attacks one, the other may escape. Not much confidence in the supernatural camps there.

Only after doing all that does Jacob start praying. Genesis tells of no reply to this prayer, though perhaps the meeting that will shortly happen counts as a response to it. In the meantime, Jacob continues to take action that arises out of his fear and again arouses at least a wry smile if not a guffaw from people listening to the story. The magnitude of the "gift" he sends ahead to Esau is monumental, a reflection of the magnitude of his fright. It is also a magnitude of the prosperity God has indeed given him over those twenty years in Paddan-aram. I guess it would not be a laughing matter to the servants who stood in the front of the firing line that Jacob is anticipating, though it is not clear how much of the dynamics of the situation they know about. When Jacob "says" that he hopes to pacify his brother with this gift, perhaps he speaks only to himself, in which case they might simply be bemused. But they must have recognized there was something odd about this whole proceeding. As a final testimony to his fear, Jacob even sends on ahead his immediate family and his personal possessions. It is as if he then stands paralyzed.

GENESIS 32:24b–33:17

God Struggles

24bAnd a man wrestled with him until daybreak, 25but saw that he had not overcome him. So he struck him at his hip socket, so that Jacob's hip socket was put out as he wrestled with him. 26He said, "Let me go away, because day has broken." Jacob said, "I will not let you go away unless you bless me." 27He said to him, "What is your name?" He said, "Jacob." 28He said, "You will no longer be called Jacob, but Israel, because you have 'striven with God' and with human beings and have overcome." 29Jacob asked, "Will you tell me your name?" He said, "Why is it that you ask my name?" But he blessed him there. 30Jacob called the name of the place Peniel saying, "Because I saw God face-to-face, but my life was saved." 31The sun rose on him as he passed Penuel. He was limping because of his hip. 32Hence the Israelites do not eat the thigh muscle that is on the hip socket, because he struck Jacob on the hip socket at the thigh muscle.

33:1Jacob looked up and saw: There, Esau was coming, and with him four hundred men. He divided the children among Leah, Rachel, and the two maidservants, 2and put the maidservants and their children first, Leah and her children after them, and Rachel and Joseph last. 3He himself went on ahead of them and bowed to the ground seven times until he came up to his brother. 4Esau ran to meet him and hugged him, threw his arms around his neck and kissed him, and they wept. 5He looked up and saw the women and the children, and said, "Who are these of yours?" He said, "The children with whom God has favored your servant." 6The maidservants came up, they and their children, and bowed low. 7Leah also came up, and her children, and bowed low. Last, Joseph came up, and Rachel, and they bowed low. 8He said, "Who are this entire camp of yours that I have met? Jacob said, "To find favor in my lord's eyes." 9Esau said, "I have much, brother. What you have must remain yours." 10Jacob said, "Please, no. If I have really found favor in your eyes, take my gift from my hand, because I have seen your face, like seeing God's face, and you accepted

115

me. ¹¹Do take my blessing which has been brought to you, because God has favored me, and because I have everything." So he urged him, and he took it.

¹²Esau said, "Let's move and go. I will go in front of you." ¹³Jacob said to him, "My lord knows that the children are frail and the flock and the cattle are suckling with me. Driven hard for one day, the entire flock will die. ¹⁴Will my lord go on before his servant? I myself will lead on gently, according to the pace of the possessions that are before me and at the pace of the children, until I come to my lord in Seir." ¹⁵Esau said, "May I place with you some of the people who are with me?" He said, "Why is it that I find favor in my lord's eyes?" ¹⁶So Esau went back that day on his journey to Seir, ¹⁷whereas Jacob moved on to Sukkot and built himself a house there and made "shelters" for his cattle. Hence the place was called Sukkot.

Every Sunday on the way to church we drive past a particular bus shelter with a huge advertising placard, and for some while this placard proclaimed, "You can never have enough money." I can't remember what it was advertising (which shows that advertising works, because I remember the placard and am extending its reach by telling you about it, but it also shows that advertising doesn't work, because I didn't notice the product the advertisement was selling). I used to think about the statement every time we passed, wondering how many people thought it was true. As I think about it now, I associate it with a scandal that has been hot in the news concerning the monumental size of the bonuses paid to some business executives, amounting to millions of dollars. And I wonder, What can a person do with all that money? When does enough become enough?

Jacob didn't know the meaning of "enough." But one useful thing about wealth, he thought, was that it should enable him to buy his way back into a peaceful relationship with his brother, at least so that he no longer wants to kill him. Jacob assumes Esau thinks the same way he does. He assumes Esau still cares about the blessing, in its material form, and he knows he has to give it back. Actually, if Esau still intended to kill Jacob, I doubt whether bribes would sort the matter out. Esau would presumably say, "Thank you very much," kill Jacob anyway, and appropriate all the rest of his assets. But Esau is interested only

116

in meeting his brother again if he can just find him as he fights his way through the camels and goats. He doesn't know what he would do with more cows and sheep and camels. He has plenty. (Unless, of course, this is simply a polite exchange, and Esau really means, "Oh, thanks!") The wonderful irony of the reunion is that Esau's four hundred men are not a posse but a welcome party of escorts. Jacob is all prostration, and Esau just wants a hug. They both weep, but the tears mean something different for Jacob from what they mean for Esau.

Allowing for the cultural differences, we can easily enough understand what is happening between Jacob and Esau, how Jacob is thinking that money can buy love and how Esau is more interested in being reunited with his long-lost brother. What was going on in the wrestling match is harder for us to comprehend, because there is unlikely to be anything in our experience that gives access to an understanding. In a way, that difficulty is symbolized by the title often given to the story. People say it is about Jacob's wrestling with God. We can then see a link with our own more figurative experiences of wrestling with God, perhaps to persuade God to let us get out of something we don't want to do. That's a useful way to use the wrestling image, though often it turns out that we are wrestling with ourselves. Jacob was no doubt also wrestling with himself in his anxiety and fear, but this isn't the story's angle, which is highlighted by the way it starts. Jacob didn't start this fight. Jacob wasn't wrestling with God. If God was involved, God was wrestling with Jacob. Actually it says that "a man" wrestled with Jacob, though it eventually does talk about Jacob's striving with God and Jacob's assuming he has seen God face-to-face, which suggests that this is another of those occasions in Genesis when God appears as a human being and only afterwards does someone realize it was more than that. All this makes it unlikely that Jacob is wrestling with himself or (in his imagination) with Esau or with a demon.

So why is God wrestling with Jacob? God has been doing that all Jacob's life, trying to turn Jacob into the man God wants him to be but failing. Here is God trying again but succeeding only by cheating, which means the victory is hollow. Perhaps one reason God appears as just a man is that this makes it a fair

117

fight. If God overwhelms us simply through having superior fire power, it's not much use as a victory. God has to "win us," as we say. We have to want to yield to God's purpose and God's vision for us if the change in us is to be authentic. But Jacob does not want to yield, and never does.

Yet God does bless him and gives him a new name that epitomizes his nature. As is often the case, the comment about the names has some subtleties about it. It links Jacob's new name with the fact that he is the great fighter. And yes indeed, Jacob is a person who keeps fighting with God in order to stay the man he is. In the end God lets him do that because even God cannot force people to change. God can only make them limp. Yet a neophyte Hebraist would know that "Isra-el" does not actually mean "he fights/persists/exerts himself with God." It is a statement of which God is the subject—as God was the initiator of the fight in the story. If anything, "Isra-el" would mean "God fights/persists/exerts himself." God strives to get a person like Jacob to become the kind of person he could be and should be and that God wants him to be, and keeps at it in this struggle with Jacob.

Once more we need to recall that the audience of this story *is* Jacob, *is* Israel. And insofar as the church comes to share in Israel's relationship with God, we recall that we too are Jacob, *we* are Israel. We are a people whose nature is to struggle with God to avoid becoming the people we could be, and a people with whom God continues to struggle to try to take us there. (The listeners might also be inclined to assume that actually the verb in this name looks more like a different one and that the name means "God rules," which also encourages some reflection.)

GENESIS 33:18–34:31

Should Our Sister Be Treated like a Whore?

[18]Jacob came peaceably to the city of Shechem, which was in the country of Canaan, as he came from Paddan-aram, and camped in front of the city. [19]He acquired the plot in the open country where he pitched his tents from the sons of Hamor,

Shechem's father, for a hundred qesitas. [20]He set up an altar there and called it "God the God of Israel."

[34:1]Dinah, the daughter whom Leah bore Jacob, went out to see the daughters of the country. [2]Shechem son of Hamor the Hivite, the leader of the country, saw her, took her, and slept with her. He forced her, [3]but his heart was stuck on Dinah, Jacob's daughter. He loved the girl, and tried to reassure her. [4]Shechem said to his father Hamor, "Get me this young woman as a wife."

[5]When Jacob heard that he had defiled his daughter Dinah, his sons were with his cattle in the open country, so Jacob remained silent until they came. [6]Hamor, Shechem's father, came out to Jacob to speak with him. [7]When Jacob's sons came from the open country on hearing about it, the men were grieved and full of fury, because he had done an outrageous thing in Israel in sleeping with Jacob's daughter. Such a thing is not done. [8]Hamor spoke with them. "My son Shechem, has fallen for your daughter. Will you give her to him as wife? [9]Make marriages with us: give your daughters to us and take our daughters for yourselves. [10]You will live among us and the country will be in front of you. Live there, move about in it, and acquire holdings in it." [11]Shechem said to her father and to her brothers, "May I find favor in your eyes: whatever you say to me, I will give. [12]Set a very large marriage payment and gift upon me, and I will give as you say to me. But give me the girl as wife."

[13]Jacob's sons answered Shechem and his father Hamor deceitfully, because he had defiled their sister Dinah. [14]They said to them, "We cannot do this, give our sister to a man who is uncircumcised, because that would be a disgrace to us. [15]Only on this basis could we consent to you, if you become like us by every male of yours being circumcised, [16]and we will give our daughters to you and we will take your daughters for ourselves, and we will live with you and we will become one people. [17]But if you will not give heed to us by being circumcised, we will take our daughter and go." [18]Their words seemed good to Hamor and Hamor's son Shechem, [19]and the young man did not delay doing the thing, because he was enchanted with Jacob's daughter. Now he was the most respected person in his father's household. [20]So Hamor and his son Shechem went to the gate of their city and spoke to the men of their city: [21]"These people are peaceable with us. They should live in the country

and move about in it; this country is wide enough for them. We will take their daughters for ourselves and give our daughters to them. ²²Only on this basis will the people consent to us to live with us to become one people, by every male of ours being circumcised as they are circumcised. ²³Their livestock and their property and all their cattle: will they not become ours? Only let us consent to them and live with them." ²⁴All the people who went to the gate of his city gave heed to Hamor and his son Shechem, and every male, all the people who went to the gate of his city were circumcised.

²⁵On the third day, when they were in pain, Simeon and Levi, two of Jacob's sons, Dinah's brothers, took each his sword, came to the city when it seemed secure and slew every male. ²⁶Hamor and his son Shechem they slew with the sword, and they took Dinah from Shechem's house and left. ²⁷Jacob's sons came upon the corpses and plundered the city because they had defiled their sister. ²⁸Their flocks, their herds, and their donkeys, what was in the city and what was in the open country, they took, ²⁹all their wealth, all their little ones, and all their women they captured and plundered, with everything that was in the houses.

³⁰But Jacob said to Simeon and Levi, "You have brought trouble on me, making me obnoxious to the people who live in the country, the Canaanites and the Perizzites. I am few in number. They will gather against me and attack me and destroy me, I and my household." ³¹But they said, "Should he have treated our sister like a whore?"

There were a couple in the seminary who got into a tangle in their relationship. The man had lost his wife in an accident. He seemed to be doing all the right things in the way he coped: grieving but keeping her memory alive, while getting on with life and trying to establish a new life pattern. The woman had never been married but wanted to be. She knew the wife and cared about her, and like the rest of us, admired the way he coped with his loss. Like other people, she tried to express her support of him in practical ways, offering him a meal or asking him out. A relationship developed, and they slept together, but then he said it had to stop because he was not in a position to commit himself to her. By this time she had much invested in her dream of a life with him, and there was a breakup that everyone knew about, with each side giving his or her version of the story. When that kind of thing happens, it's often impossible for anyone outside the relationship to understand the dynamics or the rights and wrongs. It's probably impossible for the people themselves. It's the same when a couple divorce. There are commonly two irreconcilable stories, and people outside have to be wary of thinking they understand.

The account of the way Shechem related to Dinah is quite confusing. Why does the reference to rape follow on the reference to their having sex? Does a man really fall in love with someone after raping her? Or was it more like seduction or date rape? Would he have said she went along with it? We get no account of how Dinah felt about any of it; the focus lies on where the affair led. Genesis does assume the sex was nonconsensual and that a man has no right to force or push a woman into having sex. It makes no reference to what Dinah thought about marrying Shechem, but the usual pattern suggests that a woman would not be compelled to marry a man if she didn't wish to. Yet when everyone knows the woman is not a virgin, it does not improve her marriage prospects, and the woman might assume she really had little choice but to accept the marriage that was on offer.

We can't tell the answers to those questions about what really went on between Shechem and Dinah, as we can't tell the answers to the questions about relationships we observe or even relationships we are involved in. What happens here, and what happens in our context, is that when the relationship becomes a matter of public scandal, the community has to handle it. Dinah's father knows this; Shechem's father knows it. And the old men think they have found a way of handling it that will suit everybody. Hamor and Shechem gather a town meeting in the open area at the city gate, where such meetings regularly happen and where the city's elders consult. It's a win-win situation. But again with irony, Jacob falls for his sons' deceit just as Hamor and his sons do. Hamor's name suggests the story was told in a way that took the edge off a little of its horror by humor, since it is also the Hebrew word for a female donkey. The humor has a dark side, arousing a guffaw as well as a smile: consider the picture of the poor Hivites dancing about in discomfort after their circumcision and unable to defend themselves. (There is further irony in the way some other Hivites later deceive the Israelites, in Joshua 9.)

The darkest humor is this: The descendants of Jacob-Israel are supposed to be a means of bringing blessing to the nations. They are to be an open community; anyone who wishes to join them can do so. Jacob's sons talk about their group and the Hivites becoming one people. It is a lovely vision. The Hivites just have to be circumcised. (It is odd that they were not circumcised, because most other peoples in the region were.) This is the sign of the **covenant**. But Jacob's sons turn the sign of life into a sign of death. (There is yet a further irony in the fact that it looks as if the Hivites, who lived in the hill country around Shechem and to the south and northeast of there, also eventually become assimilated into Israel so that the two do become one people, though with Israel dominant, which was not the scenario Hamor envisaged.)

GENESIS 35:1–29

Do People Change?

[1]God said to Jacob, "Set off and go up to Bethel. Live there and make an altar there to the God who appeared to you when you were fleeing from your brother Esau." [2]So Jacob said to his household and to all who were with him, "Get rid of the alien gods that are in your midst. Purify yourselves. Change your clothes. [3]We shall set off to go up to Bethel and make an altar there to the God who answered me on the day of my distress and has been with me on the way that I have traveled." [4]They gave Jacob all the alien gods that they possessed, and the rings that were in their ears, and Jacob buried them under the terebinth that was near Shechem. [5]As they moved on, a supernatural terror came over the cities that were round about them, and they did not pursue the sons of Jacob. [6]So Jacob came to Luz, which was in the country of Canaan (that is, Bethel), and all the people that were with him. [7]He built an altar there and called the place "God of Bethel," because God had appeared to him there when he was fleeing from his brother. [8]Deborah, Rebekah's nanny, died, and was buried below Bethel under the oak. So it was called Weeping Oak.

⁹God appeared to Jacob again when he came from Paddan-aram, and blessed him. ¹⁰God said to him, "Your name is Jacob. You will no longer be called Jacob, but Israel will be your name." Thus he named him Israel. ¹¹God said to him, "I am El Shadday. Be fruitful and numerous. A nation and a community of nations will come into being from you. Kings will come out of your loins. ¹²The country that I gave to Abraham and Isaac I will give to you, and I will give the country to your offspring after you." ¹³God went up from him at the place where he spoke with him, ¹⁴and Jacob set up a stone pillar and poured out a libation on it and poured oil on it. ¹⁵Jacob named the place where God spoke with him Bethel.

¹⁶They moved on from Bethel. They were still a distance from reaching Ephrath and Rachel gave birth. She had a hard time in giving birth. ¹⁷When she was having a hard time in giving birth, the midwife said to her, "Don't be afraid, because this, too, is a son for you." ¹⁸As her breath left her, because she was dying, she called him "Son of my Trouble"; but his father called him "Son of my Right Hand." ¹⁹So Rachel died and was buried on the road to Ephrath (that is, Bethlehem). ²⁰Jacob set up a pillar at her grave (it is the pillar at Rachel's grave to this day). ²¹Israel moved on and pitched his tents beyond Migdal Eder. (²²While Israel was staying in that region, Reuben went and slept with Bilhah, his father's secondary wife, and Israel took heed.)

Jacob's sons were twelve. ²³Leah's sons: Jacob's firstborn, Reuben; Simeon; Levi; Judah: Issachar; and Zebulun. ²⁴Rachel's sons: Joseph and Benjamin. ²⁵The sons of Bilhah, Rachel's maidservant: Dan and Naphtali. ²⁶The sons of Zilpah, Leah's maidservant: Gad and Asher. These are Jacob's sons who were born to him in Paddan-aram.

²⁷Jacob came to his father Isaac at Mamre at Kiriath Arba (that is, Hebron), where Abraham and Isaac stayed. ²⁸Isaac was a hundred and eighty years old. ²⁹Isaac breathed his last and died and joined his kin, old and sated with years. His sons Esau and Jacob buried him.

We used to meet each week for dinner with a group of friends, including a pastor or two, a therapist or two, and a missiologist or two, and one of the topics we used to come back to was transformation. Mission is concerned with it; ministry is concerned with it; therapy is concerned with it. I used to get into trouble for saying I wasn't sure I believed in it. Admittedly, I eventually realized, part of the problem was that for me (and I think in Britspeak) "transformation" implies something much more radical than "change," whereas the words were more similar in meaning for the others. Maybe I could believe in change. That still raises the question, In what sense do we believe people change? Coming to know Christ allegedly means a radical change in the orientation of a person's life, but it does not in practice make people oriented to being more concerned for others than for themselves. Certainly it should surely not be expected that conversion, healing, growth toward maturity, or growth in holiness turns introverts into extraverts. What about anxious people into laid-back people? Or people attracted to the same sex into people attracted to the opposite sex? I know I am more of a people-person than I used to be, and I suspect it is at least in part somehow a result of having to live with my wife's illness. I also know I am more mellow than I used to be, but is that just the result of growing older?

Does Jacob change? Is Jacob transformed? Did that meeting with God at the river Jabbok change him? The way he approached Esau afterward doesn't make it look like it. Here, once again Genesis 35 tells us about Jacob's being renamed Israel. But the change of name does not seem to imply a change of personality.

It is also surprising to find another account of Jacob's change of name here. It is another example of the way Genesis often includes two versions of an event—two creation stories, two accounts of God's **covenant** with Abraham, and so on. It reflects the way the author of Genesis was not starting from scratch in telling the story of things that happened centuries before the author's day but preserving traditions that had been passed down in the community, as well as developing them, and hesitating to throw anything away. In this chapter, virtually everything is familiar; virtually everything has come before. So what the chapter does is provide a kind of reminder, reprise, and summary of where we have been, though with distinctive notes of it own.

As far as one can see, Jacob is not transformed. This does not mean **El Shadday** has given up on him, nor on his sons. With

124

God, hope springs eternal. We do not change, and we carry on making the same mistakes, but this does not make God throw up hands in despair and abandon us. Jacob's move from Shechem to Bethel took him only a short distance down the mountain chain, but it takes him to a place associated with God rather than with the shameful events of the previous chapter, and giving up the "alien gods" fits with that. It is a surprise to find that the family has alien gods, though they are likely not as bad as they sound but more like Rachel's **effigies**; in fact, they would include them (we don't know the point about the earrings, but maybe they had similar associations). And although Jacob is not transformed (in the Britspeak sense), his action as they move to Bethel does suggest a renunciation of what we might call natural religion. The story will again bring its encouragement and its challenge to the Jacob-Israel that listens to this story. It can be encouraged that God does not give up on it, even though it is not transformed. On the other hand, it is challenged to give up the natural religion that it was continually inclined to combine with its theoretical commitment to the God who made these promises to the original Jacob-Israel and is still committed to keeping them.

After a while the family sets off for the south, where Isaac still lives (and maybe Rebekah; Genesis does not record her death). On the way, Rachel bears the family's twelfth son. She chooses a name for him that matches what has happened; Jacob insists on a different name. Is it an insensitive refusal to own the way the love of his life gave her life for his twelfth son, in the way women often do in traditional societies? Or is it a grieved inability to be reminded of that fact every time he speaks to this child? Or is it a proper commitment to living for the future in light of God's promise? Rachel's grave sits there on the way south (though some confusion obtains about exactly where it was) as a place of weeping when **Judeans** go off into **exile** (Jeremiah 31:15) and when Jesus is born (Matthew 2:16–17).

The sordid note about Reuben indicates how he was positioning himself as successor to his father; he was the eldest son yet not the son of the most loved wife, so who knows what will happen. . . . But his initiative will rebound on him. The close of the chapter recalls the death of Abraham, and it neatly has Esau and Jacob together at this moment as Isaac and Ishmael had been at Abraham's death.

GENESIS 36:1–37:4

Excluded but Not Forgotten

¹This is the line of Esau (that is, Edom). ²Esau took his wives from the daughters of Canaan: Adah daughter of Elon the Hittite, Oholibamah daughter of Anah daughter of Zibeon the Hivite, ³and Basemath daughter of Ishmael, sister of Nebaioth. ⁴Adah bore Eliphaz for Esau, Basemath bore Reuel, ⁵and Oholibamah bore Jeush, Jalam, and Korah. These are the sons of Esau who were born to him in the country of Canaan. ⁶Esau took his wives, his sons, and his daughters, and the people in his household, his cattle, all his livestock, and the property that he had acquired in the country of Canaan and went to a country away from his brother Jacob, ⁷because their possessions were too great for them to live together and the country where they were staying could not support them because of their livestock. ⁸So Esau lived in the mountains of Seir (Esau is Edom).

⁹These are the names of Esau's sons: Eliphaz, son of Esau's wife Adah; Reuel, son of Esau's wife Basemath. ¹¹The sons of Eliphaz were Teman, Omar, Zepho, Gatam, and Kenaz. ¹²Timna was a secondary wife to Esau's son Eliphaz; she bore Amalek for Eliphaz. These were the descendants of Esau's wife Adah. ¹³These were the sons of Reuel: Nahath, Zerah, Shammah, and Mizzah. These were the descendants of Esau's wife Basemath. ¹⁴These were the sons of Esau's wife Oholibamah, daughter of Anah daughter of Zibeon: she bore Esau Jeush, Jalam, and Korah.

¹⁵These are the chiefs of the descendants of Esau. The descendants of Esau's firstborn, Eliphaz: the chiefs Teman, Omar, Zepho, Kenaz, ¹⁶Korah, Gatam, and Amalek. These are the chiefs of Eliphaz in the country of Edom; these are the descendants of Adah. ¹⁷These are the descendants of Esau's son Reuel: the chiefs Nahath, Zerah, Shammah, and Mizzah. These are the chiefs of Reuel in the country of Edom; these are the descendants of Esau's wife Basemath. ¹⁸These are the descendants of Esau's wife Oholibamah: the chiefs Jeush, Jalam, and Korah. These are the chiefs of Esau's wife Oholibamah, daughter of

Anah. [19]These are the descendants of Esau and these are their chiefs (that is, Edom).

[20]These are the sons of Seir the Horite who were living in the country: Lotan, Shobal, Zibeon, Anah, [21]Dishon, Ezer, and Dishan. These are the chiefs of the Horites, the sons of Seir, in the country of Edom. [22]The sons of Lotan were Hori and Hemam; Lotan's sister was Timna. [23]These are the sons of Shobal: Alvan, Mahanath, Ebal, Shepho, and Onam. [24]These are the sons of Zibeon: both Aiah and Anah (he was the Anah who found the hot springs in the wilderness when he was pasturing the donkeys of his father Zibeon). [25]These are the children of Anah: Dishon and Anah's daughter Oholibamah. [26]These are the sons of Dishan: Hemdan, Eshban, Ithran, and Cheran. [27]These are the sons of Ezer: Bilhan, Zaavan, and Akan. [28]These are the sons of Dishan: Uz and Aran. [29]These are the chiefs of the Horites: the chiefs Lotan, Shobal, Zibeon, Anah, [30]Dishon, Ezer, and Dishan. These are the chiefs of the Horites according to the chieftainships in the country of Seir.

[31]These are the kings who reigned in the country of Edom before a king reigned over the Israelites: [32]Bela son of Beor reigned in Edom; the name of his city was Dinhabah. [33]When Bela died, Jobab son of Zerah from Bozrah reigned instead of him. [34]When Jobab died, Husham from the country of the Temanites reigned instead of him. [35]When Husham died, Hadad son of Bedad, who defeated Midian in the region of Moab, reigned instead of him. The name of his city was Avith. [36]When Hadad died, Samlah from Masrekah reigned instead of him. [37]When Samlah died, Shaul from Rehoboth-on-the-river reigned instead of him. [38]When Shaul died, Baal-hanan son of Achbor reigned instead of him. [39]When Baal-hanan son of Achbor died, Hadar reigned instead of him. The name of his city was Pau, and his wife's name was Mehetabel daughter of Matred daughter of Me-zahab.

[40]These are the names of Esau's chiefs according to their clans and places, by their names: the chiefs Timna, Alvah, Jetheth, [41]Oholibamah, Elah, Pinon, [42]Kenaz, Teman, Mibzar, [43]Magdiel, and Iram. These are the chiefs of Edom according to their settlements in the country that is their holding (that is Esau, Edom's ancestor).

[37:1]Jacob lived in the country where his father had stayed, the country of Canaan. [2]This is Jacob's line. Joseph, when he was seventeen years old, was pasturing the flocks with his brothers; he was a boy with the sons of his father's wives Bilhah and Zilpah. Joseph brought a bad report about them to their father. Now Israel loved Joseph most of all his sons, because he was the son of his old age. He made an ornamented coat for him. ⁴His brothers saw that their father loved him more than all his brothers, and they were not able to speak a peaceable word to him.

Some years ago I decided to try to discover what I could about the Goldingays of the past. It's probably easier for most British people to investigate their ancestors than for most people in the United States, whose families came from a different continent. So I have (for instance) a copy of the marriage certificate of John Goldingay, who married Sarah Massey in 1841 in the same parish where this John Goldingay lived just over a century later. The certificate does not give their ages; it simply says they were "of age," over twenty-one and free to make their decision about marrying. Sarah was a brickmaker, and she could not write; she just made her mark on the certificate. John was already a widower, and I wonder about the story behind that. Until I write this, I guess few people have thought much about John and Sarah over the past century or so. As Ecclesiastes comments, we are born, we die, we are forgotten.

It is a strange fact that the Israelites ensured that so many of Esau's family did not get totally forgotten. It is strange because we have noted in connection with Genesis 27 that there was no more love lost between Israel and Edom than there was between Jacob and Esau in their youth. At least, the Old Testament (especially the Prophets) tells us how negatively Israel felt about Edom, and we know how much of **Judah**'s land fell into Edomite control later in Old Testament times. Yet Genesis knows Edom is somehow part of God's story, even if less central than Israel. As happened with Ishmael and Isaac, Genesis tells us about the descendants of the older son before telling us about those of the younger son, because it is the latter on whom the story is to focus. The same pattern begins to assert itself when Genesis turns to Jacob's line and notes Jacob's favoritism toward his young son Joseph, which does not thrill his big brothers.

But Israel could never dismiss Ishmael's line or Esau's line. One of the most chilling of the Prophets' statements about Edom comes at the beginning of Malachi, where God declares, "I have loved Jacob but hated Esau" (Malachi 1:2). Admittedly that literal English translation may be misleading. Jesus will later declare that people need to hate their parents if they are to follow him, indicating a practical commitment to put one relationship over another rather than mere negative feelings, and Malachi implies something similar. But Paul is not embarrassed by Malachi's words when he quotes them in Romans 9:13. One reason is that God's positive action in relation to Israel as opposed to Edom is all part of God's project of redeeming the whole world. What Genesis adds to this is a declaration that Edom itself does matter. Its story is part of God's story.

The account gives a further illustration of the way Esau has mellowed, whether or not Jacob has done so. The story of Esau and Jacob recapitulates the story of Abraham and Lot as well as that of Ishmael and Isaac. Once again there is not enough room in the country for both households. It is a sign of their flourishing, of their experiencing God's blessing. And it is Esau who takes the initiative and moves south and east to the country that becomes Edom. It is also a sign of God's blessing that Edom generates not merely chiefs but kings, a fulfillment of God's promise to Abraham (Genesis 17:6), and one that comes about before God fulfills the same promise to Jacob (Genesis 35:11).

GENESIS 37:5–36

The Dreamer

⁵Joseph had a dream and told his brothers, and they hated him some more. ⁶He said to them, "Will you listen to this dream that I have had? ⁷There—we were binding sheaves in the middle of the country. There—my sheaf got up, yes, stood. There—your sheaves gathered around and bowed down to my sheaf." ⁸His brothers said to him, "Are you really going to reign over us? Will you really rule over us?" They hated him some more because of his dreams and what he said. ⁹He had another dream and told it to his brothers. "There—the sun and the moon and eleven stars were bowing down to me." ¹⁰He told his father and

his brothers, and his father reprimanded him and said to him, "What is this dream that you have had? Are your mother and your brothers and I going to bow down to the ground to you?" [11]So his brothers were incensed at him, while his father kept the matter in mind.

[12]His brothers went to pasture their father's flocks at Shechem. [13]Israel said to Joseph, "You know your brothers are pasturing the flocks at Shechem? Come on, I will send you to them." He said to him, "I'm here." [14]Israel said to him, "Will you go and see if all is well with your brothers and with the flocks, and bring back word to me?" So he sent him from the vale of Hebron. He came to Shechem [15]and a man found him: he was wandering about in the open country. The man asked him, "What are you looking for?" [16]He said, "I am looking for my brothers. Can you tell me where they are pasturing?" [17]The man said, "They have moved from here, because I heard them say, 'Let's go to Dothan.'" So Joseph followed his brothers and found them at Dothan. [18]They saw him from a distance, and before he got near them they plotted to put him to death. [19]They said one to another, "Here: that great dreamer is coming! [20]So now, come on, let's kill him and throw him into one of the cisterns. We'll say a wild animal ate him. We'll see what will become of his dreams." [21]But Reuben heard them and rescued him from their power. He said, "We won't take his life."

[22]So Reuben said to them, "Don't shed his blood. Throw him into this cistern in the wilderness. Don't lay a hand on him" (so that he might rescue him from their power and give him back to his father). [23]So when Joseph came to his brothers, they stripped Joseph of his coat, the ornamented coat that was on him, [24]took him, and threw him into the cistern. The cistern was empty; there was no water in it.

[25]They sat down to have dinner, but looked up and saw: there, a caravan of Ishmaelites coming from Gilead, their camels carrying spices, balm, and myrrh, on the way to take them down to Egypt. [26]Judah said to his brothers, "What's the gain if we kill our brother and cover up his blood? [27]Come on, let's sell him to the Ishmaelites. Our hands—they shouldn't be on him, because he is our brother, our flesh and blood." His brothers gave heed. [28]So when some Midianite traders passed by, they pulled Joseph and got him up out of the cistern. So they sold Joseph to the Ishmaelites for twenty silver pieces, and they took Joseph to

130

Egypt. ²⁹Reuben came back to the cistern, and there—Joseph was not in the cistern. He tore his clothes ³⁰and went back to his brothers and said, "The boy isn't there! And I—where can I turn?" ³¹They took Joseph's coat, slaughtered a goat, dipped the coat in the blood, ³²and sent the ornamented coat to get it to their father, and said, "We found this. Will you look at it? Is it your son's coat, or not? ³³He recognized it and said, "My son's coat! A wild animal has eaten him! Joseph has been torn to pieces!" ³⁴Jacob tore his clothes, put sackcloth around him, and mourned for his son for a long time. ³⁵All his sons and daughters set about comforting him, but he refused to be comforted and said, "I will go down to Sheol to my son mourning." So his father wept for him.

³⁶Meanwhile the Medanites sold him to the Egyptians, to Potiphar, an officer of Pharaoh, the chief guard.

I have known one or two people who had dreams or visions or words from God (indeed, I have had one or two myself). Sometimes these have been rather general and uncheckable, though edifying and at worst harmless. Sometimes they have been vindicated by events or confirmed in some other way. Sometimes they have left me thinking, "Yes, well, he or she would think something like that. Saying it is a word from God just gives spurious authority to what is essentially just that person's thinking." I particularly remember an angry prophet who was angry and bitter even when he was not prophesying. Annoyingly, however, those words that seem simply to reflect the humanity of the dreamer, the visionary, or the prophet can also be edifying, or (worse still) can be vindicated by events or confirmed in some other way. Just because it is the kind of thing this person would say doesn't exclude the possibility that God is involved in the saying of it.

There is a related ambiguity about Joseph's dream. When we start reading the story, there is no hint here that it is a God-given dream, and our modern instinct is to read it psychologically. Here is teenage Joseph living in the shadow of ten (!) grown-up brothers (and who knows how many big sisters!) and their three mothers (none of whom is his, because she has died). And maybe he knows he is his aged father's favorite, but how does that help? So he dreams of being top dog, just as his father wanted to be when he had only one brother to contend with. And he is so naive, he tells everyone his silly dreams. Has journaling not been invented? (Answer: No.) And it almost costs him his life. It gives his brothers a chance to show they have their father's genes: they are as good at deceit as he is. Once again deceitfulness catches up with Jacob, who was sometimes beaten at his own game by his cousin and by his wife, and in his dotage is now beaten at it by his sons. Yet the irony is that Joseph's dreams will come true. In one sense, that is not surprising. It is how someone in this cultural context would expect things to work out. The Old Testament never refers to dreams as a purely human or psychological phenomenon; it refers to them only as something of supernatural significance.

But that is to anticipate; the dream hangs over all that we read in the coming chapters. The question is *how* will it come true, especially when events are such as surely to take the destiny of Joseph in quite other directions. But having a hunch that we know where the story has to go helps us see the significance of events as they unfold. Not untypically, human waywardness and fortunate coincidence play a part in its development. While one cannot blame the older brothers for regarding Joseph as more than a little tiresome, understanding does not extend to tolerating the cynical ruthlessness of their action.

The Middle Eastern climate means people need ways of conserving water for the dry season, so they collect it in large cisterns, a little like wells. There is something mafia-like about the way the brothers throw Joseph into the empty cistern to die, then coolly settle down for dinner. It seems strange that Judah's recognition that "he is our flesh and blood" does not extend to hesitation about selling him into slavery (twenty silver pieces is the price of a slave, and we are not talking about the relatively beneficent temporary debt servitude that the **Torah** allowed). And it seems strange that this recognition does not extend to hesitation over putting Jacob through his terrible grief, though perhaps the brothers were glad to get back at their father for making Joseph their favorite. The convenient coincidence is the fortuitous arrival of a camel caravan.

Over the following chapters, Genesis will frequently speak of going "down" to Egypt and then back "up" to the hill country of Canaan. It is puzzling that the caravan is referred to first as Ishmaelite, then as Midianite, then as Medanite. Maybe this again reflects the combining of different versions of the story. But "Ishmaelites" seems here to refer not to Ishmael's physical descendants but to people involved in trade, so that Midianite can be a subset of Ishmaelite (we know from Genesis 25 that Midian was not a descendant of Ishmael but of another of Abraham's wives). And translations usually assume that Medanite is a textual slip for Midianite (in Genesis 25, Medan was Midian's brother).

GENESIS 38:1–30

Another Deceiver Deceived

[1] At that time Judah went down from his brothers and pitched his tent near a certain Adullamite whose name was Hirah. [2] Judah saw there the daughter of a certain Canaanite whose name was Shua. He took her and slept with her. [3] She became pregnant and bore a son, and called him Er. [4] She became pregnant again and bore a son, and called him Onan. [5] Once more she became pregnant and bore a son, and called him Shelah. He was at Chezib when she bore him.

[6] Judah took a wife for his firstborn, Er. Her name was Tamar. [7] But Er, Judah's firstborn, displeased Yahweh, and Yahweh let him die. [8] Judah said to Onan, "Sleep with your brother's wife. Be a brother-in-law to her. Raise up offspring for your brother. [9] But Onan knew that the offspring would not be his, and when he slept with his brother's wife he would waste it on the ground so that he would not give offspring to his brother. [10] What he did displeased Yahweh, and Yahweh let him die. [11] Judah said to his daughter-in-law Tamar, "Live as a widow in your father's household until my son Shelah grows up," because (he thought), "He may also die like his brothers." So Tamar went and lived in her father's household.

[12] Time went on, and Shua's daughter, Judah's wife, died. When Judah had got over it, he went up to the men who were shearing his flock, he and his friend Hirah the Adullamite, to Timnah.

133

[13]Tamar was told, "Here: your father-in-law is coming up to Timnah for the shearing of his flock." [14]Tamar set aside her widow's clothes from upon her, covered herself with a veil and disguised herself, and sat at the entrance to Enaim, which is on the road to Timnah, because she saw that Shelah had grown up but she had not been given to him as wife. [15]Judah saw her and thought she was a prostitute, because she had covered her face. [16]He turned aside to her by the road and said, "Here, can I sleep with you?" because he did not know that it was his daughter-in-law. She said, "What will you give me if you sleep with me?" [17]He said, "I myself will send a kid goat from the flock." She said, "If you give me a pledge until you send it." [18]He said, "What pledge shall I give you?" She said, "Your seal and cord and the staff that's in your hand." So he gave them to her and slept with her, and she became pregnant by him.

[19]She set off and went her way, and set aside her veil from upon her and put on her widow's clothes. [20]Judah sent the kid goat by the hand of his friend the Adullamite, to get the pledge from the hand of the woman, but he could not find her. [21]He asked the people of her place, "Where is that hooker, the one at Enaim, by the road?" But they said, "There has been no hooker here." [22]He went back to Judah and said, "I couldn't find her. Moreover, the people of the place said, 'There has been no hooker here.'" [23]Judah said, "She can have it, otherwise we will be a laughingstock. Now. I sent her the kid goat, but you couldn't find her."

[24]About three months later, Judah was told, "Tamar your daughter-in-law has been immoral. In fact, yes, she is pregnant through being immoral." Judah said, "Bring her out. She should be burned." [25]As she was being brought out, she sent to her father-in-law, "It is by the man to whom these belong that I am pregnant," and said, "Will you examine them? Who is the one who owns the seal and the cord and the staff?" [26]Judah examined them and said, "She is in the right, not me, because of the fact that I did not give her to my son Shelah." He did not sleep with her again. [27]When the time of her giving birth came, there—twins were in her womb. [28]When she was giving birth, one put out a hand, and the midwife took a red thread and tied it on his hand, saying, "This one came out first." [29]But when he took back his hand, his brother came out, and she said, "What a breakout you have made for yourself!" So he was called Break-

out. ³⁰Afterward his brother, who had the red thread on his hand, came out. He was called Shining.

It can seem as if every month some new sexual scandal is reported involving a prominent politician or pastor. It is common for the men (it's nearly always men, but the more equal the playing field becomes, the more it may become women) initially to deny that anything untoward has been going on. It seems that somehow we think we can get away with anything, that we are covered in Teflon, nothing will stick to us. But then hard evidence emerges and denial no longer works. There are TV camera shots of wives standing by their man (while other wives wonder why they do that). There are professions of sorrow and repentance that seem a little too slick (well, a lot too slick) and seek to clear the way for an attempt at a comeback after a suitable (but short) withdrawal from public life.

Once again deceit plays a key role in the story of **Judah** and Tamar. Judah's living separately from the brothers parallels the way Reuben was not always with them in the previous chapter and will relate to the demands of shepherding the flocks and sometimes needing to separate in order to find pasture for them. Adullam and Timnah are southwest of Jerusalem and thus quite some distance from where the brothers have been based at Shechem. If Judah gets based there, it is not surprising for him to marry a local girl, though Genesis has emphasized the way Isaac and Jacob did not do that. We don't know how Judah's first son "displeased" God and died, though Genesis may simply mean that he died young and that God must have allowed this.

The point lies in where the story leads. Judah assumes the convention that has been common in many cultures and will be accepted in Israel, that when a man dies without children, something needs to be done to keep the man's memory alive, keep his family going, provide a destiny for his inheritance, and produce offspring to look after his widow as she grows older. (Tamar can go back to live with her parents, but most people don't regard that as an exciting long-term prospect.) So his brother is expected to marry, or at least sleep with, his widow in the hope that she can have a child who will count as her husband's. Onan doesn't mind sleeping with his sister-in-law, but he doesn't want to father her child. It is in his interest for her not to have a son; his brother's inheritance will then fall to Onan. (His action has sometimes been assumed to refer to masturbation or coitus interruptus as a regular method of birth control, but this misses the point.) He ends up also dying young. Judah is then afraid that there is a kind of curse on his family. His wife's death would not exactly discourage that suspicion, and Tamar suspects he will never get his youngest son to do his duty to her. So she devises her clever plan that takes advantage of the sexual frustration of a man whose wife dies when he still has natural sexual instincts and makes it possible for her to get pregnant.

"American Express will do nicely, thank you," says the "private dancer" in Mark Knopfler's song with that name, but Judah has no credit card and has to surrender the seal with which he signs contracts, the cord on which it hangs around his neck, and his cane, which was presumably also marked in a way that identified it as his. When people infer that Tamar has become pregnant through "acting immorally," they use the word that means "prostitute," but it has this broader connotation, and they would likely be assuming simply that she had been sleeping around. Judah's reaction illustrates the double standard that men are capable of showing and/or the projection that takes a tough stance towards the kind of action that we know we ourselves are guilty of or tempted to. That is underlined by the toughness of the action he proposes (despite the terms the **Torah** will later use, there are no instances of anyone being executed for any sexual misdemeanor in the Bible).

On the other hand, Judah's comment when he is found out shows he has faced up to the facts. He makes a beautifully succinct statement that provides a model for us twenty-first century men when we fall. "She is in the right, not me." He does add a reason: "I did not give her to my son Shelah." But he does not turn that into an excuse. His being scared has been mentioned earlier, but here Judah refers to his action, not his fear; it constitutes the reason he is guilty, not an appeal to extenuating circumstances.

Once again we are astonished and encouraged that stories with all the messiness of our stories are there in the Bible. And this is the man who gives his name to one of Israel's most important clans, the one from which David and Jesus are born; and this is the Tamar who appears in Jesus' genealogy (Matthew 1:3).

GENESIS 39:1–40:8

God Was with Joseph

[1]So Joseph had been taken down to Egypt and a certain Egyptian, Potiphar, an officer of Pharaoh, the chief guard, had acquired him from the hands of the Ishmaelites who had taken him down there. [2]But Yahweh was with Joseph and he became a successful man. He was in the household of his Egyptian master, [3]and his master saw that Yahweh was with him and that everything that he was doing, Yahweh made succeed in his hand. [4]So Joseph found favor in his eyes and served him, and he put him in charge of his household and put into his hands everything that belonged to him. [5]From the time that he put him in charge of his household and everything that belonged to him, Yahweh blessed the Egyptian's household because of Joseph. Yahweh's blessing was on everything that belonged to him, in the house and outside. [6]He left everything that he had in Joseph's hands, and with him, he did not pay attention to anything except the food that he was eating.

Joseph became handsome and good-looking, [7]and after all this his master's wife looked at Joseph and said, "Sleep with me." He refused, and said to his master's wife, "Now. With me, my master does not pay attention to what is in the house. Everything that belongs to him he has put in my hands. [9]He is not greater in this household than me. He has not kept back from me anything except you, because you are his wife. How could I commit this great wrong and offend against God?" [10]Though she spoke to Joseph day after day he did not give heed to her by sleeping with her or being with her. [11]On such a day he went into the house to do his work. None of the people of the household was there in the house. [12]She caught hold of him by his coat, saying, "Sleep with me," so he left his coat in her hand, fled, and went outside. [13]When she saw that he had left his coat in her hand and fled outside, [14]she called the people of the household and said to them, "Look, he brought us a Hebrew man to fool about with us! He came to me in order to sleep with me and I called out in a loud voice, [15]and when he heard me raising my voice and calling out, he left his coat with me and fled, and went outside." [16]She placed his coat with her until his master came home, [17]and spoke to him in the same words: "The Hebrew servant whom you brought to us came to me in order to fool about with me, [18]and when I raised my voice and called out he left his coat with me and fled outside."

[19]When his master heard the words that his wife spoke to him, "These are the things that your servant did to me," he was furiously angry. [20]Joseph's master took him and put him in the jailhouse, the place where the king's prisoners were imprisoned. So he was there in the jailhouse, [21]but Yahweh was with Joseph and kept commitment to him, and gave him favor in the eyes of the jailhouse officer. [22]The jailhouse officer put into Joseph's hands all the prisoners who were in the jailhouse, and everything that was being done there, he was the one doing it. [23]The jailhouse official did not look at any matter in his hands, because Yahweh was with him and whatever he was doing Yahweh made succeed.

[40:1]After these things happened, the king of Egypt's cupbearer and baker offended their master the king of Egypt. [2]Pharaoh was angry with his two officers, the chief cupbearer and the chief baker, [3]and put them under guard in the house of the chief guard in the jailhouse, the place where Joseph was imprisoned. [4]The chief guard put Joseph with them and he served them. They were some time under guard, [5]and the two of them had a dream, the king of Egypt's cupbearer and baker who were imprisoned in the jailhouse, each his own dream, the same night, each dream with its own interpretation. [6]Joseph came to them in the morning and saw that they were vexed. [7]He asked Pharaoh's officers who were with him under guard in his master's house, "Why are your faces grim today?" [8]They said to him, "We had dreams, and there is no one to interpret them." Joseph said to them, "Do interpretations not belong to God? Will you tell me them?"

I previously referred to a man who used to come to talk with me when he had an affair and was inclined to blame the women for throwing themselves at him. But I have known women who were tempted to do that. Sometimes their men were totally pre-occupied, and they felt neglected; indeed, they were neglected. In another instance, a woman's husband had a chronic illness, and it was all he could think about. There was a woman whose husband was simply boring, and there was a man who seemed to be throwing himself at her, making compliments about her appearance, looking as if he was interested in her. Maybe he was, or maybe it was her imagination. Likewise, maybe the man who reckoned women were throwing themselves at him was giving too much scope to his imagination. Maybe it was wish fulfillment. Whether you are the man or the woman, the person inclined to wander or the person who feels someone is showing an interest in you, it may be impossible to know and impossible to raise the question ("Excuse me, I just wondered whether you were angling for an affair . . .").

When we read Joseph's story, we may be inclined to won-der about the woman's version of what happened. Would she say that as he grew up this hot guy was flaunting his muscles around the house, asking for it? We certainly pick up hints that her husband is clueless. All he cares about is his work and what's for dinner.

So the story is a melodramatic tale about a handsome young man, a stupid husband, and a lonely wife. But another element in the story is the involvement of God, and linking these two aspects of it is wisdom. Stereotypical characters such as these are the staple of the teaching in Proverbs. Proverbs is concerned to help young men avoid getting entangled with the "strange woman," a phrase that can suggest both the "other woman," the woman who doesn't mind having an affair, and a foreign woman, somebody from outside the community or someone who may have different mores or religion and lead one astray. Potiphar's wife makes the category on both scores, but Joseph deals with sexual temptation or sexual instincts in a very dif-ferent way from Judah.

God was with Joseph. God had promised to be with his father and his grandfather (see Genesis 26 and 28) and had kept that promise. It is fulfilled for Joseph, too. As was the case for them, this means God made things work out well for him; it did not merely mean he had a feeling that God was with him.

As William Tyndale's old translation put it, "The Lord was with Joseph and he was a lucky fellow." Further, it means he sees some fulfillment of God's promise to his great grandfather that he would be a means whereby blessing came to other peoples (see Genesis 12). Through Joseph, blessing comes to the Egyptians among whom he lives and works.

It certainly looks as if the idea that God was with Joseph collapses when he ends up in jail, yet Genesis then takes up that idea again. Joseph is the guy who keeps bouncing back, not because he has an inherent resilience but because God is with him and shows **commitment** to him. Joseph ends up in the same position of responsibility in the jail as the one he held with Potiphar.

Much later in the Old Testament story, Joseph's finding favor with Potiphar and then with the jailor is a motif that finds a parallel in the story of Daniel in his relationship with a senior royal official (see Daniel 1:9). Daniel will be in a similar position in Babylon to Joseph's in Egypt, a captive in a foreign country. Is it possible to get through that experience? Is it even possible to do well in that context? Both stories promise their audience that if they go through that experience (as many do) it is possible both to survive and to do well. Their challenge is to stay faithful to what they know is right. The invitation to them is to live in hope that "God will be with you" even when things go horribly wrong. It does not always work out, but it *can* work out.

GENESIS 40:9–41:24

When You Need an Expert

[9]So the chief cupbearer told Joseph his dream. He said to him, "In my dream: there, a vine was in front of me. [10]On the vine were three branches. Even as it budded, its blossom came out and its clusters ripened as grapes. [11]Pharaoh's cup was in my hand, and I got the grapes, pressed them into Pharaoh's cup, and placed the cup into Pharaoh's hand." [12]Joseph said to him, "This is the interpretation. The three branches are three days. [13]In three days' time Pharaoh will lift up your head and put you

back in your position. You will place Pharaoh's cup in his hand in accordance with the former practice when you were his cupbearer. [14]Only be mindful of me when things go well for you. Will you keep commitment with me and make mention of me to Pharaoh so that you get me out of this house? [15]Because I was actually stolen from the country of the Hebrews, and also I have done nothing here that they should have put me in the dungeon."

[16]The chief baker saw that the interpretation was good and said to Joseph, "In my dream, also: There, three wicker baskets were on my head. [17]In the top basket there were all kinds of food for Pharaoh, the work of a baker. But birds were eating it from the basket on my head." [18]Joseph answered, "This is the interpretation. The three baskets are three days. [19]In three days' time Pharaoh will lift up your head from on you and impale you on a tree, and the birds will eat your flesh from on you."

[20]On the third day, Pharaoh's birthday, he made a banquet for all his servants, and lifted up the head of the chief cupbearer and the head of the chief baker among his servants. [21]He put the chief cupbearer back into his position, and he placed the cup in Pharaoh's hand, [22]but the chief baker he impaled, as Joseph interpreted to them. [23]But the chief cupbearer was not mindful of Joseph. He disregarded him.

[41:1]Two years later, Pharaoh dreamed. There, he was standing by the Nile. [2]There, from the Nile seven cows were coming up, lovely in appearance and sturdy in body, and they grazed among the reeds. [3]And there: seven more cows were coming up from the Nile after them, poor in appearance and lean in body, and they were standing beside the cows on the bank of the Nile. [4]The cows that were poor in appearance and lean in body ate the seven cows that were lovely in appearance and sturdy. And Pharaoh woke up. [5]He went to sleep and dreamed a second time. There: seven ears of grain were growing on a single stalk, sturdy and good quality. [6]And there: seven ears that were thin and scorched by the east wind were springing up after them. [7]The thin ears swallowed the seven sturdy, full ears. And Pharaoh woke up. There: it was a dream.

[8]In the morning his spirit was agitated, and he sent and summoned all Egypt's diviners and all its experts. Pharaoh told them his dream, but no one could interpret them for Pharaoh. [9]The chief cupbearer spoke with Pharaoh: "I am making mention of

my offenses today. [10]When Pharaoh was angry with his servants, he put me under guard in the house of the chief guard, me and the chief baker. [11]We had dreams the same night, he and I. Each of us dreamt in accordance with the interpretation of his dream. [12]With us there was a Hebrew lad, a servant of the chief guard. We told him and he interpreted our dreams to us, to each of us the interpretation according to his dream. [13]And as he interpreted it to us, so it came about. I was put back into my position and he was impaled." [14]So Pharaoh sent and summoned Joseph, and they hurried him from the dungeon. He shaved and changed his clothes, and came to Pharaoh. [15]Pharaoh said to Joseph, "I had a dream and no one can interpret it. I have heard about you, that when you hear a dream, you can interpret it." [16]Joseph replied to Pharaoh, "Not me. God is the one who will respond with well-being for Pharaoh."

[17]Pharaoh spoke with Joseph. "In my dream: there, I was standing by the bank of the Nile. [18]And there, from the Nile seven cows were coming up, sturdy in body and lovely in appearance, and they grazed among the reeds. [19]And there, seven more cows were coming up after them, lean and very poor in appearance, thin in body. I have not seen the like of them in all the country of Egypt for poorness. [20]The thin, poor cows ate the first seven sturdy cows [21]and they went down inside them but it would not have been recognized that they had gone down inside them. Their appearance was as poor as it was at the beginning. Then I woke up. [22]Then I saw in my dream, and there—seven ears of grain coming up on one stalk, full and good quality; [23]and there—seven ears of grain springing up after them, withered, thin, scorched by the east wind. [24]And the thin ears swallowed the seven good ears. I talked with the diviners but no one could tell me."

Three months ago, I had a routine medical procedure (I will spare you the clinical details). A few weeks before it was due, I happened to read a report of research on this particular procedure that suggested it might not be as useful as has been assumed for decades. The report outlined the factors involved in determining whether it was a good idea or not and concluded that sometimes it could be worse than useless. So should people have the procedure or not? The report concluded, as such reports often do, that these were facts that patients needed to take into account in coming to a decision. Yeah, thanks. The report reflected our culture's fascination with "the latest research." We assume that the facts are out there and that if we investigate them we can solve every problem; and this assumption has proved fruitful. Yet each week one can read of research that conflicts with the basis on which previous research encouraged people to make decisions. The old Woody Allen film *Sleeper* portrays its hero asleep for decades, then waking up to find that everything that was supposed to be bad for you (such as smoking) turns out to be good for you, and vice versa. We need and long for the information that will enable us to live our lives in wise ways, but is the information possible to find?

In ancient Egypt an equivalent to scientific research was dream research. We have Egyptian examples of dream books listing motifs that recur in dreams and what they "mean." If you dream about a well, or about weaving, or about looking at yourself in a mirror, or about thousands of other things, these could portend something good or bad that was going to happen. While such guidance might be general, it could point to some specific future event. But dreams reveal the future only in an oblique way. You need to know how to interpret them. In Egypt there were unofficial and officially recognized dream experts who could help ordinary people interpret their dreams.

Whereas Joseph is in prison despite the fact that he has resisted the temptation to "offend against God" (Genesis 39:9), Pharaoh's chief cupbearer and chief baker have "offended" their boss. We don't know how they did so. The perils of life in a Middle Eastern court may mean only that the fish pie was not spicy enough. In their troubled situation in prison and their anxiety about what the future may hold, they assume there should be something to learn from their dreams, but they do not have a dream book or a dream expert handy; at least, so they assume. But Joseph asks the rhetorical question that both undermines their natural assumption about dreams and promises that they might be able to find a way forward: "Do interpretations not belong to God?" Our touching faith in modern research needs to have set alongside it the limitations in what empirical research can discover. Its findings are always provisional, and they themselves need interpretation. We cannot sell our souls to research or think we can save our bodies through research.

It may be even more dangerous that our culture also sees research as the key to politics. We spend millions on "intelligence" yet continually make decisions about involvement in other nations' affairs that turn out to have been misguided. We had lots of information, but we lacked a big picture and we lacked wisdom. Pharaoh had all those resources, but his experts were baffled by his dreams. At least they had the brave humility to admit it. If we lack a Joseph, as we usually do, we would at least be wise to face the limitations of our resources.

GENESIS 41:25–57

Save First, Spend Afterward

[25]Joseph said to Pharaoh, "Pharaoh's dream is just one. God has told Pharaoh what he is going to do. [26]The seven good cows are seven years and the seven good ears of grain are seven years. It is just one dream. [27]The seven thin and poor cows that were coming up after them are seven years, as are the seven thin ears of grain, scorched by the east wind. There will be seven years of famine. [28]That is the thing I am declaring to Pharaoh. God has shown Pharaoh what he is going to do. [29]Now. Seven years are coming, great abundance in all the country of Egypt, [30]but seven years of famine will arise after them, and all the abundance in the country of Egypt will be forgotten. The famine will consume the country, [31]and the abundance in the country will not be recognized in the face of that famine afterwards, because it will be very severe. [32]Concerning the repeating of the dream to Pharaoh, twice: the thing is fixed by God. God is going to do it quickly. [33]And now, Pharaoh should identify a man of insight and expertise and set him over the country of Egypt. [34]Pharaoh should act and appoint commissioners over the country and take a fifth of the country of Egypt in the seven years of abundance. [35]They should collect all the food in these good years that are coming and lay up the grain in the cities as food, under the control of Pharaoh. [36]The food will be a reserve for the country for the seven years of famine that are going to happen in the country of Egypt so that the country is not cut off by the famine."

[37]The proposal seemed good to Pharaoh and all his servants, [38]and Pharaoh said to his servants, "Shall we find a man like this, in whom is the spirit of God?" [39]So Pharaoh said to Joseph, "Since God has made all this known to you, there is no one of insight and expertise like you. [40]You yourself will be over my household, and to your word all my people will acquiesce. Only with respect to the throne will I be greater than you." [41]So Pharaoh said to Joseph, "See, I am putting you over all the country of Egypt." [42]Pharaoh removed his signet ring from on his hand and put it on Joseph's hand, had him clothed in linen robes, and put a gold chain on his neck. [43]He had him ride in the chariot of his second-in-command, and they called out before him, "Bow down!" So he put him over all the country of Egypt. [44]Pharaoh said to Joseph, "I am Pharaoh, but without you no one will raise his hand or his foot in all the country of Egypt."

[45]Pharaoh called Joseph Zaphenath-paneah and gave him Asenath, daughter of Potiphera, priest in Heliopolis, as wife. So Joseph went out over the country of Egypt. [46]Now Joseph was thirty years old when he began to serve Pharaoh, the king of Egypt. Joseph went out from before Pharaoh and traveled through the whole country of Egypt. [47]In the seven years of abundance, the country produced to overflowing, [48]and he collected all the food of the seven years that passed in the country of Egypt and put the food in the cities; the food of a city's countryside that was around it he put in its midst. [49]Joseph laid up the grain like the sand of the sea in huge amounts until he stopped accounting, because accounting was impossible.

[50]Two sons were born to Joseph before the famine year came; Asenath daughter of Potiphera, the priest in Heliopolis, bore them for him. [51]Joseph called the firstborn Manasseh, because "God has made me 'forget' all my trouble and all my father's household." [52]The second he called Ephraim, because "God has made me 'fruitful' in the country of my affliction."

[53]The seven years of abundance that passed in the country of Egypt came to an end [54]and the seven years of famine began to come, as Joseph had said. The famine happened in all the countries, but in all the country of Egypt there was food. [55]So when all the country of Egypt was hungry and the people cried out to Pharaoh for food, Pharaoh said to all the Egyptians, "Go to Joseph, do what he says." [56]When the famine was over all the face of the country, Joseph opened all that was in them and

sold grain to the Egyptians. So the famine became severe in the country of Egypt, [57]while the whole world came to Egypt to Joseph to buy grain, because the famine was severe in the whole world.

Writers and TV producers have noted that the cell phone and other technological devices have undermined some of the staple plot devices that make novels and movies work. In *Casablanca*, Rick need not have been in any doubt as to why Ilsa stood him up at the train station in Paris; she would have sent him a message. No one ever needs to get lost; they have GPS. A news report concerning this effect of technology on novels and movies gave Joseph as an example: he could have dialed for help from the cistern. So if Joseph had owned a cell phone, Judaism would not have existed, a reporter commented. (Admittedly, this might not seem to follow, though there might have been no need for an exodus, which is a pretty far-reaching consequence.) More immediately, Joseph would not be in a position to have to make his plaintive comments about missing his family: "God has made me forget all my trouble and all my father's household." Just call them, Joseph.

But his comment surely deconstructs. How can it be true that God has made him forget all his trouble and all his father's household if he is talking about it when his eldest son is born and if this son's name (which looks almost like a form of the word "forget") is always going to be reminding him of it? Later episodes in this story will also make clear that neither in a good sense nor in a bad sense has he forgotten his father or what his brothers did to him. The same point emerges from his second son's naming, as once again he refers to his "affliction."

For people listening to the story, the account of the two boys' births will have a further significance. Manasseh and Ephraim became two of the most significant Israelite clans, dominating the northern part of the country. Once Israel split into two after Solomon's day, **Ephraim**, indeed, often appears as the name of the northern of the two nations. Yes, God made Joseph fruitful. Ephraim's own name could remind people of this because of its overlap with the word for "be fruitful." Joseph's not having a cell phone might not have prevented the emergence of Judaism, but it would have reworked Israel's history in another way if these two sons had never have been born.

For one of Jacob's youngest sons to be the forefather of these two significant clans is typical of God's working in Genesis. To put two and two together, the stories in Genesis 35 and 38 have implied that Reuben and **Judah** have ruled themselves out of seniority in the family by their sexual behavior. Joseph has not done so. On the other hand, surprisingly the author of Genesis has no problem with Joseph's wife being the daughter of a priest at the great city of Heliopolis, Sun City, where the sun god was the focus of worship. Perhaps Egyptian religion was seen as less of a threat or temptation than **Canaanite** religion. In general the Old Testament shows less unease about insight from Egypt than about insight from Canaan.

The recession that began in 2008 came about in large part as a result of our living beyond our means for years. Our motto has been "Spend first, save later." If you can make things work out the opposite way, it has advantages. Joseph's interpretation of Pharaoh's dreams makes it possible to save first and then manage through the crisis when it comes. Joseph surely didn't have to be a genius to formulate a plan to handle what was to unfold over the periods of surplus and shortage. Yet with hindsight one can say that likewise the world doesn't have to get into the economic messes it gets into from time to time. One big factor that generates them is a combination of greed and stupidity; more specifically, greed makes people throw wisdom to the winds. The years of prosperity could have made Egypt do that. Joseph shows them how to stay cool and take the longer view. We might reckon it is not surprising that someone who lives by God's promises and by trust in God would have the kind of insight to see the wise basis on which to run the country's economic policies in years of plenty and in years of lack. On the other hand, there will in time be a downside to the "big government" that Joseph suggests. The actual factor that makes Pharaoh put Joseph in charge of implementing his economic policies is not so much the innovative nature of his proposals but the supernatural insight indicated by his ability to interpret dreams. It leads Pharaoh to identify Joseph as the first person in Scripture in whom the spirit of God is at work. Wisdom is a gift of God's spirit, to be desired in any ruler.

GENESIS 42:1–35

What Game Is Joseph Playing?

[1]Jacob saw that there was grain in Egypt. So Jacob said to his sons, "Why do you look at each other?" [2]He said, "Now. I have heard that there is grain in Egypt. Go down there and buy grain for us from there so we may live and not die." [3]So ten of Joseph's brothers went down to buy grain from Egypt; [4]As for Joseph's brother Benjamin, Jacob did not send him with his brothers, because (he said) disaster might come to him. [5]So Israel's sons came to buy grain among the people who came because the famine happened to the country of Canaan. [6]Now Joseph was the prime minister over the country. He was the one who sold grain to all the people of the country. So Joseph's brothers came and bowed down to him, their faces to the ground. [7]Joseph saw his brothers and recognized them, but acted like a stranger to them and spoke harshly with them. He said to them, "Where have you come from?" They said, "From the country of Canaan, to buy food."

[8]So Joseph recognized his brothers but they did not recognize him. [9]And Joseph recalled the dreams that he had about them. Joseph said to them, "You are spies. You have come to see the country's vulnerability." [10]They said to him, "No, my lord! Your servants, they have come to buy grain. [11]We are all of us sons of one man. We are honest men. Your servants have not been spies." [12]He said to them, "No, you came to see the country's vulnerability." [13]They said to him, "Your servants, we were twelve brothers, the sons of one man in the country of Canaan, but now: the youngest is with our father at the moment, and one is no more." [14]But Joseph said to them, "It is as I stated it to you: 'You are spies.' [15]By this you will be tested: By the life of Pharaoh, you will not leave here unless your youngest brother comes here. [16]Send one of you to get your brother, and you will be imprisoned, to test your words, whether there is truth in you. Otherwise, by the life of Pharaoh, you are spies."

[17]He imprisoned them under guard for three days. [18]On the third day, Joseph said to them, "Do this and you will live; I revere God. [19]If you are honest, one of your brothers must be imprisoned in your guard house while you go and take grain for the famine in your households, [20]and your youngest brother you shall bring to me so that your words may be shown to be

148

true and you may not die." So they did that, 21and said to each other, "Really, we are paying the penalty for our brother. We looked at the distress that filled him when he pleaded for favor with us and we didn't listen. That's why this trouble has come upon us." 22And Reuben responded to them, "Didn't I say, 'Don't offend against the boy?' and you didn't listen? Yes, his blood—there, it is being required." 23Now, they did not know that Joseph was listening, because there was an interpreter between them. 24He turned away from them and wept, but came back to them and spoke to them, and took Simeon from among them and imprisoned him before their eyes. 25But Joseph gave orders that their bags were to be filled with grain, each man's money was to be put back into his sack, and they were to be given provisions for the journey.

So he did this for them; 26they loaded their grain onto their donkeys, and went from there. 27One of them opened his sack to give feed to his donkey at the lodging and saw his money. There it was, in the mouth of his bag. 28He said to his brothers, "My money has been put back! Really, here it is, in my bag!" Their heart sank. They turned trembling to one another, saying, "What is this that God has done to us?" 29They came to their father Jacob in the country of Canaan and told him all that had happened to them. 30"The man who is lord of the country spoke harshly with us and treated us as people who were spying out the country. 31We said to him, 'We are honest. We have not been spying. 32We were twelve brothers, the sons of our father; one is no more and the youngest is with our father in the country of Canaan at the moment.' 33But the man who is lord of the country said to us, 'By this I shall know that you are honest. Leave one of your brothers with me and take something for the famine in your households, and go, 34and bring your youngest brother to me, so that I may know that you are not spies but are honest. I will give your brother to you and you can move about in the country.'" 35As they were emptying their sacks, there—each man's money pouch was in his sack. They and their father saw the money pouches, and were afraid.

I arrived home late one evening, picked up the mail, and checked messages. When I was in charge of a seminary, I used to avoid reading messages just before bedtime in case it gave me things to worry about that kept me from sleeping, but I don't usually need that rule now. On this occasion, however, a publisher had sent a clutch of reviews of something I had written, including a strangely negative one from another Old Testament professor. Usually negative reviews don't bother me much. I can often see that the person simply has a different perspective from mine (or is young and keen to make a mark). This review didn't convince me that I should have written a different book, but it did feel hurtful because the basis for the negativity seemed odd and I would have counted the reviewer a friend. Why was *he* being so harsh? Was he keen not to be influenced by our acquaintance? Had he had a bad day? What was going on in his life? What was his motivation for writing like that (other scholars have reviewed the book favorably)? Have I offended him in some way? Or was it simply that on this subject he had a different perspective from mine? Was it my problem? Am I too easily hurt? (Answer: yes. It's a little like student evaluations. As one of my colleagues put it, if we read forty-nine positive evaluations and one negative evaluation, it is the negative one that sticks.) Maybe I should have called him, but I didn't. So his words remain a mystery to me.

Joseph is a mystery throughout this story. For several chapters he will be playing games with his brothers and his father, and/or the author of Genesis will be playing games with us. When Joseph named Manasseh, he said he had forgotten about his brothers and his suffering, but this is hardly so. And it will be hard to tell why he is playing games with his brothers. Is it because he needs to draw them to genuine repentance for the wrong they have done, and because they need to be pushed lower and lower into remorse and shame before it will be wise to let them rise from it? I have had an occasion in my own life when that was so. Centuries later, God will reckon Israel needs to be taken into the shame of **exile** and left to wallow there for some while in the shame of humiliation and rejection by God before it will be wise to restore them. "What is this that God has done to us?" they ask. Are they serious enough yet about the question, or are they asking it in the profound sense in which it needs asking?

Or is Joseph playing games with his brothers because he has some resentment in his heart for what his brothers did to him as a teenager in selling him into servitude, exiling him from his family and his homeland, and (indirectly) causing him to end up in prison through no fault of his own? It would be understandable if he has some simmering resentment and if in his naming of Manasseh he is simply kidding himself about having forgotten it all.

If we were able to ask him which of these motivations impels him, perhaps he would not know. If he deserves his reputation as a person of insight, he might be wise to acknowledge the possibility that both motivations drive him and that he is not sure which is dominant. And if we could ask God's opinion about what is going on, perhaps God would reckon that the brothers do need to be brought to a deep and genuine repentance, that the way Joseph is treating them does have the capacity to bring this about, and that even if Joseph's resentment is driving him more than it should—well, God works through human weakness and sin as well as through human strength and righteousness (as Joseph himself will eventually point out).

Reuben had successfully urged his brothers not to spill Joseph's blood, but perhaps they had refrained from doing that only in a technical sense. As far as they knew, they had effectively terminated his life. He surely had no life worth living after they sold him into slavery, and Reuben cannot help but assume that his blood is now being required of them.

GENESIS 42:36–43:34

What Game Is Genesis Playing?

[36]Their father Jacob said to them, "I am the one you have bereaved of children. Joseph is no more and Simeon is no more and you are going to take Benjamin. It has all happened to me." [37]But Reuben said to his father, "You may kill my two sons if I do not bring him back to you. Put him into my responsibility and I myself will bring him back to you." [38]But he said, "My son is not to go down with you, because his brother is dead and he alone is left. If disaster comes to him on the journey that you are taking, you will send my gray hair down to Sheol with grief."
[43:1]But the famine in the country was severe. [2]When they had finished eating the grain that they had brought from Egypt,

their father said to them, "Go back and buy us a little more food." [3]But Judah said to him, "The man solemnly affirmed to us, 'You shall not see my face unless your brother is with you.' [4]If you do send our brother with us, we will go down and buy food for you. [5]But if you do not send him, we will not go down, because the man said to us, 'You shall not see my face unless your brother is with you.'" [6]Israel said, "Why did you bring trouble to me by telling the man you had another brother?" [7]They said, "The man asked a lot about us and about our family, saying, 'Is your father still alive? Do you have a brother?' and we told him these things in response. Could we possibly know that he would say, 'Bring your brother down here?'" [8]Judah said to his father Israel, "Send the boy with me so we can set off and go, and live and not die, we and you and our little ones as well. [9]I personally guarantee him. From my hand you can require him. If I do not bring him back to you and set him before you, I will have offended against you forever. [10]Because if we had not delayed, we could by now have got back here twice." [11]Their father Israel said to them, "If it is so, then, do this. Get some of the country's products in your bags and take them down to the man as a gift: a little balm and a little honey, spices and myrrh, pistachios and almonds. [12]And take twice the money with you, take back with you the money that was put back in the mouth of your bags. Perhaps it was a mistake. [13]And your brother: take him and set off and go back to the man. [14]May El Shadday himself give you compassion before the man so that he may release your other brother to you, and Benjamin. And me—when I am bereaved, I am bereaved." [15]So the men took this gift and took twice the money with them, and Benjamin, and set off and went down to Egypt and stood before Joseph.

[16]Joseph saw Benjamin with them and said to the person over his household, "Take the men into the house and slaughter an animal and prepare it, because the men will eat with me at noon." [17]The man did as Joseph said, and the man brought the men into Joseph's house. [18]The men were afraid because they were brought into Joseph's house. They said, "It is because of the money that was put back in our bags the first time that we have been brought in, to overwhelm us and overpower us and take us as slaves, and our donkeys." [19]So they approached the man who was over Joseph's house and spoke to him at the entrance to the house. [20]They said, "Pardon me, my lord, we

only came down the first time to buy food. [21]But when we came to the lodging, we opened our bags and there: each man's money was in the mouth of his bag, our money by its weight. We have brought it back with us [22]while we have brought down other money with us to buy food. We don't know who put our money in our bags." [23]He said, "All is well with you. Don't be afraid. Your God, the God of your father, gave you the treasure in your bags, as your money came to me." And he brought Simeon out to them. [24]So the man took the men into Joseph's house, gave them water to wash their feet, and gave them feed for their donkeys. [25]They prepared the gift for when Joseph came at noon, because they had heard that they were to have a meal there.

[26]So Joseph came home and they gave him the gift that they had with them in the house, and bowed down to him to the ground. [27]He asked them whether things were well, and said, "Is it well with your aged father of whom you spoke? Is he still alive?" [28]They said, "It is well with your servant, our father. He is still alive," and made obeisance and bowed down. [29]He looked and saw his brother Benjamin, his mother's son, and said, "Is this your youngest brother of whom you spoke to me?" And he said, "God show favor to you, my son." [30]Then Joseph hurried out because his affection was so strong for his brother and he needed to weep, so he went to a room and wept there. [31]He washed his face and came out and controlled himself and said, "Serve the meal." [32]They served him by himself and them by themselves and the Egyptians who ate with him by themselves, because the Egyptians could not eat a meal with the Hebrews because this would be an offense to Egyptians. [33]They sat before him, the firstborn according to his birthright and the youngest according to his youth. The men looked in astonishment at one another. [34]Portions were brought from before him to them, but Benjamin's portion was bigger than the portions of all of them, five times. They drank and were merry with him.

In the movie *The English Patient*, Count Laszlo crashes a plane and in order to go to get help has to abandon the only woman he has loved, in an injured state, in a cave in a desert mountain. He is long unable to convince people to listen to him. When he eventually returns, she has died. He gathers his love's body and carries it around the mountain to where he had landed his plane, crying a scream that we see on his lips but do not hear, so that it all the more fills the cinema with its silence. That was the scene in the movie that most affected me, but I discovered this reaction to be a male perspective. Not surprisingly, a woman with whom I discussed it found the most emotionally engaging moment to be the one when the woman, left to die alone in the cave, tries to draw a final picture while daylight diminishes and darkness and cold descend. You can walk home with friends after a movie and discover you have all seen different things, and you may disagree vehemently about what it meant. A movie's nature is often to leave gaps for the audience to fill, and we fill them in light of who we are.

That also happens in biblical stories. In Genesis, not only is Joseph playing games with his brothers, but the author of Genesis is playing games with the people listening to the story. We cannot be sure of the answer to the questions about Joseph's motivation; in the end, that is between Joseph and God. The effect of the story's unclarity is to put the ball into our court and make us examine ourselves. If I were Joseph, what would be my motivation? What do I learn from the way I read the story? Paradoxically, often the Bible works on us by leaving things unclear, making us fill in the gaps, and then asking why we fill them in the way we do.

Among the ironies of the story is the way Jacob is affected as well as the brothers who were directly responsible for Joseph's being in Egypt. "I am the one you have bereaved of children," he says. Joseph, Simeon, Benjamin: when will it stop? The grievous aspect to the irony is that Jacob is having to lie in the bed he has made; his favoritism towards Joseph as his first son by his favorite wife played a key role in events that followed. Yet he made his bed the way he did because of his own family background. Readers of Exodus are offended by the suggestion that the sins of parents are visited on their children to the third and fourth generation, but one does not have to read the Bible to learn that it is so. Yet the Bible does provide one or two spectacular illustrations of how this works out, and Jacob is one of them. The way Genesis tells the story, we cannot attribute all of Jacob's troubles to the way Isaac and Rebekah related to him

154

and his brother, but neither can they be absolved of some of the responsibility. Jacob pays the penalty for who his parents were. In turn, his sons pay the penalty for the person their father was. They too become experts at deception and victims of deception. And Jacob becomes the victim of their deception—both that of Joseph and that of his brothers. He goes through a bereavement over which he grieves for years when actually his son, the elder son of the woman he really loved, is still alive.

GENESIS 44:1–34

Tough Love

[1]He instructed the person over his household, "Fill the men's bags with food, as much as they can carry, and put each person's money in the mouth of his bag. [2]And my chalice, the silver one, put in the mouth of the bag of the youngest, with his grain money." He acted in accordance with the word that Joseph said. [3]When morning dawned and the men had been sent off, they and their donkeys, [4]they had left the city without going far when Joseph said to the person over his household, "Set off and chase after the men. Catch up with them and say to them, 'Why have you repaid wrong for good? [5]Isn't this the one that my master drinks from and he practices divination with? You have done wrong in the way you acted.'" [6]So he caught up with them and spoke these words to them. [7]They said to him, "Why does my lord speak words such as these? Far be it from your servants to do such a thing as this. [8]Now. The money that we found in the mouth of our sacks we brought back to you from the country of Canaan. So how could we steal silver or gold from your master's house? [9]Whoever of your servants it is found with, he will die, and also we will become slaves to my lord." [10]He said, "Yes, in accordance with your words, so it shall now be: whoever it is found with, he will be a slave to me. But you will be free from blame." [11]They hastened, each man, to lower his bag to the ground, and they opened, each man, his bag, [12]and he searched, beginning with the eldest and ending with the youngest. And the chalice was found in Benjamin's bag. [13]They tore their clothes, and they loaded, each man, his donkey and went back to the city.

[14]So Judah and his brothers came to Joseph's house. He was still there. They fell on the ground before him. [15]Joseph said to

them, "What is this deed that you have done? Did you not know that a man like me practices divination?" [16]Judah said, "What can we say to my lord? What can we speak? How can we show we are in the right? God has found out your servants' waywardness. Here we are, slaves to my lord, both we and the one in whose possession the chalice was found." [17]But he said, "Far be it from me to do this. The man in whose possession the chalice was found: he will become a slave to me. You: go up in peace to your father." [18]Judah approached him and said, "Pardon me, my lord, can your servant speak a word in my lord's ear and your anger not flame up at your servant, because you are like Pharaoh. [19]My lord asked your servants, 'Do you have a father or mother?' [20]and we said to my lord, 'We have an aged father and the child of his old age, the youngest. His brother is dead, and he alone remains of his mother's, and his father loves him.' [21]You said to your servants, 'Bring him down to me so that I can set my eye on him.' [22]We said to my lord, 'The boy cannot abandon his father. If he abandons his father, he will die.' [23]But you said to your servants, 'If your youngest brother does not come down with you, do not let me see your faces.' [24]When we went up to your servant my father, we told him my lord's words. [25]And when our father said to us, 'Go back, get a little food for us,' [26]we said, 'We cannot go down unless our youngest brother is with us so that we can go down, because we will not be able to see the man's face with our youngest brother not being with us.' [27]Your servant my father said to us, 'You yourselves know that my wife bore me two sons. [28]One went from me and I said, "Yes, he has been torn to pieces." I have not seen him since. [29]If you take this one from my presence as well and disaster comes, you will send my gray hair down to Sheol with trouble.' [30]If I now come to your servant my father and the boy is not with us, given that his life is bound up with his life, [31]when he sees the boy is not there, he will die. Your servants will send your servant my father's gray hair down to Sheol with grief. [32]Because your servant guaranteed the boy to my father, saying, 'If I do not bring him back to you, I will have offended against my father forever.' [33]So may your servant now live as a slave to my lord instead of the boy. The boy must go up with his brothers. [34]Because how can I go up to my father with the boy not with me? I must not behold the woe that will come on my father."

A woman came to see me the other day. She thought she had met the love of her life. I had seen her with him. There had developed that light that comes into people's eyes when they know they are loved. They had started talking about engagement. But then something made her suspect that all was not well, and she had confronted her boyfriend about what might have happened when he went on a trip back east, when she knew he would be seeing a woman with whom he had had a relationship going back to their teenage years. This other woman was still keen on him; and he admitted that he had not only seen her but had slept with her, and that it was not the first time he had done so since the relationship allegedly ended some years ago. I imagined that the woman wanted to come to talk to me about her sense of hurt and grief, but actually she wanted to discuss more specifically something that was both theological and practical in the context. What did forgiveness mean in these circumstances? At one level the answer was obvious. It was her job not to hold a grudge against her boyfriend, not to harbor any resentment against him, to be willing to continue to view him with love. But he wanted to resume the relationship with her, and what she wanted to know was whether forgiveness meant being willing to take the risk of his behaving the same way again. There is no end to love's trust, hope, or endurance (1 Corinthians 13:7). Yet if she took that risk, opening herself to the possibility of being devastated by his doing the same thing again, was she perhaps failing actually to be loving to him? Was she making it too easy for him?

If we assume Joseph is not simply trying to exact revenge from his brothers, we can see him as handling this same dilemma: trying to combine a willingness to forgive with a rigor in seeking to get his brothers to face the facts about what they have done. They have to be driven deeper into shame and into owning the implications of what they did years ago if they are to find true maturity and find reconciliation with their brother.

The story would have challenging though indirect implications for many of its readers. In the story, the lead brothers are Judah on one side and Joseph on the other. After Israel (that is, Jacob's descendants) divided into two nations dominated by **Judah** and by the Joseph clans, relations between them were sometimes cordial but were often strained or adversarial. It was odd that the two parts of the family of Jacob were thus divided. The story of this relationship between their forebears points them towards a realism that does not hide from issues that need to be faced, but also to an openness to and desire for family reconciliation. The people of God can never be satisfied with enmity within the family.

For the third time here, the brothers prostrate themselves before Joseph. They obviously would not make a link with the dreams of Joseph that set this story going, but presumably Joseph did so, as presumably would people listening to the story. The brother's action fulfills the bumptious, annoying little brother's dream of their sheaves bowing down to his. This does not alter the fact that it was an expression of his brashness. Nor does it quite establish that it was God-given in the way Jacob's own dream of the stairway to heaven had been. As is the case with the question of Joseph's motivation for the way he treats his brothers, Genesis does not quite connect the dots over the dream's status. It thereby leaves Joseph, the brothers, and the story's audience in the same position in which we often find ourselves. We don't always know the answer to questions like that and have to live our lives on the basis of partial insights. But we can do that in the conviction that Joseph will shortly express, that God is involved in the whole story even if we cannot be sure of the significance of even key elements within it.

GENESIS 45:1–28

Not You but God

[1]But Joseph could not control himself before all the people who were attending on him. He proclaimed, "People are to leave my presence, everyone!" So no one was there with him when Joseph made himself known to his brothers, [2]but he cried out as he wept; the Egyptians heard and Pharaoh's household heard. [3]Joseph said to his brothers, "I'm Joseph! Is my father still alive?" His brothers could not answer him because they were terrified at his presence. [4]Joseph said to his brothers, "Do come near to me," and they came near. He said, "I'm your brother

Joseph, whom you sold into Egypt. [5]Now. Don't be distressed, don't let it make you angry at yourselves because you sold me here, because it was to save life that God sent me ahead of you. [6]Because this has been two years of famine within the country, and there will be five more years with no plowing and reaping. [7]God sent me ahead of you to establish for you a body of survivors in the country, to save life for you for a great escape group. [8]So now it was not you who sent me here but God. He has established me as a father to Pharaoh and as lord of all his household and ruler over all the country of Egypt. [9]Hurry and go up to my father and say to him, 'Your son Joseph has said this, "God has established me as lord of all Egypt. Come down to me, don't wait. [10]You will live in the region of Goshen and be near me, you and your children and your grandchildren, your flocks, your cattle, and all that is yours. [11]I will provide for you there because there will be five more years of famine, so that you and your household and all that is yours does not become dispossessed."' [12]Here: your eyes can see and my brother Benjamin's eyes can see that it is my mouth that is speaking to you. [13]You are to tell my father about all my honor in Egypt and all that you have seen, and hurry up and bring my father down here." [14]He threw his arms round his brother Benjamin's neck and wept, and Benjamin wept on his neck, [15]and he kissed all his brothers and wept on them, and after that his brothers spoke with him.

[16]When the story was heard in Pharaoh's household, "Joseph's brothers have come," Pharaoh and his servants were pleased. [17]Pharaoh said to Joseph, "Say to your brothers, 'Do this: Load your animals and set off, go the country of Canaan. [18]Get your father and your households and come to me. I will give you the best of the country of Egypt and you will eat the fat of the land. [19]You are instructed, do this: take for yourselves from the country of Egypt wagons for your little ones and wives, and transport your father and come. [20]Your eye is not to look with sadness at your belongings, because the best of all the country of Egypt will be yours.'"

[21]Israel's sons did so. Joseph gave them wagons in accordance with Pharaoh's word and gave them provisions for the journey. [22]To them all he gave a change of clothing for each person, and to Benjamin he gave three hundred pieces of silver and five changes of clothing. [23]To his father he sent as follows: ten

donkeys carrying some of the best things of Egypt, and ten she-donkeys carrying grain, food, and provisions for their father for the journey. [24]Then he sent his brothers off, and as they went, he said to them, "Don't be agitated on the way." [25]So they went up from Egypt and came to the country of Canaan to their father Jacob [26]and told him, "Joseph is still alive, and yes, he is ruler over all the country of Egypt." His heart went numb, because he did not believe them. [27]But they repeated to him all the words that Joseph had spoken to them, and he saw the wagons that Joseph had sent to transport him, and the spirit of their father Jacob came alive. [28]Israel said, "Great! My son Joseph is still alive! I must go and see him before I die!"

Last night we had a group of students in our home for dessert after class. One of them asked what is my favorite book in the Bible (the answer is Ecclesiastes) and then what is my disabled wife's favorite book. I am not aware that she ever had one, but she had a favorite text, which is that "for people who love God, he makes all things work together for good, for people who are called according to his purpose" (Romans 8:28). It is quite a statement for someone who knew she had a potentially devastating illness but didn't know that she would end up year after year unable to do anything or even to speak. Thinking about it now, I realize Paul's words have different implications from the ones I would have realized a decade or two ago. What I see in Ann is that being called according to God's purpose means being called to a role within God's wider purpose; it does not refer merely to her individual relationship with God. In her disability she has a strange ministry to people (including me), a kind of calling. God brings good out of the bad thing that is her disability.

Joseph is the first great embodiment of Romans 8:28. While his experience in Egypt brings good to him in the power and prestige it gives him, it is at least debatable whether that makes it worthwhile to be thrown into the cistern, sold into servitude in a foreign country, and put into jail. But the good that God brings out of these experiences is not merely the good it brings to Joseph (even in the possible maturing of his character) but the good it brings to his family. And that is not the end of it. The point is that this is the family through which God is going to bring blessing to the world. It is important to keep this family alive rather than letting the famine starve it to death, because they are called according to God's purpose in a special sense. We as twenty-first-century readers owe our salvation to the fact that God kept this family alive (so that Jesus could be born from it) and uses Joseph's suffering to that end. If you are Joseph, then, God's doing such an extraordinary thing through your suffering is what compensates for what you went through. It is a pattern that will be repeated in Jesus' story.

Joseph does not mean it literally when he says it was not his brothers but God. They did send Joseph to Egypt, but the Bible assumes that events can sometimes be described at more than one level. That, too, will happen in the Jesus story. On the first Pentecost after Jesus' resurrection, Peter declares that "this man, handed over by the set plan and foreknowledge of God, by means of lawless people you crucified and killed" (Acts 2:23). God knows about the human weaknesses that will make Gentiles and Jews collaborate to get rid of Jesus, and God makes that the way of executing a plan to redeem the world.

Joseph refers to God's using the brothers' action to keep alive "a body of survivors." He thus introduces into the Bible a term that will be of great significance for many people hearing the story. The expression is usually translated "a remnant." It denotes the people who go through some catastrophe but live to tell the tale. Specifically, it comes to denote those who survive the destruction of the people by Babylon centuries later. It is an expression that initially conveys bad news; the people who survive are only leftovers. But it can imply good news; at least some people survive who can be the nucleus of a renewed and restored people. God promises that this restoration will indeed come about, even in a foreign country such as Egypt (or Babylon). They can even be a great "escape group," another term used of the people who survive the later destruction of Israel. The promise that people will survive is already anticipated and fulfilled in what happens to Jacob's family back in Genesis.

God knows about the human weaknesses that will make Joseph dream about lording it over his big brothers and make the brothers give in to the temptation to get him for it, and

God makes these the means of providing the whole family with a way of surviving the famine and thus of keeping in existence the family through whom God has promised to bless the world. Those aspects of God's intention are far more important than the human weakness and wrongdoing through which God implements this purpose. Seeing that makes it possible for Joseph to live with the way his brothers have treated him, as they make it possible for Christians to accept the role that Judas, Pilate, the Jewish leaders, or the Roman soldiers played in Jesus' death.

GENESIS 46:1–34

Call No One Happy until They Are Dead

[1]So Israel made the journey with all that was his and came to Beersheba. He offered sacrifices to the God of his father Isaac, [2]and God said to Israel in a vision at night, "Jacob, Jacob!" He said, "I'm here." [3]He said, "I am God, the God of your father. Don't be afraid of going down to Egypt, because I will establish you there as a great nation. [4]I myself will go down with you to Egypt and I will also definitely bring you up from there, when Joseph closes your eyes." [5]So Jacob set off from Beersheba. Israel's sons transported their father Jacob, their little ones, and their wives on the wagons that Pharaoh had sent to transport him, [6]and got their livestock and the wealth that they had acquired in the country of Canaan, and Jacob and all his offspring with him came to Egypt. [7]His sons and his grandsons with him, his daughters and his granddaughters, and all his offspring, he brought with him to Egypt.

[8]These are the names of the descendants of Israel who came to Egypt, Jacob and his descendants. Jacob's firstborn, Reuben. [9]Reuben's sons: Enoch, Pallu, Hezron, and Carmi. [10]Simeon's sons: Jemuel, Jamin, Ohad, Jachin, Zohar, and Saul, the son of a Canaanite woman. [11]Levi's sons: Gershon, Kohath, and Merari. [12]Judah's sons: Er, Onan, Shelah, Perez, and Zerah (but Er and Onan had died in the country of Canaan); Perez's sons were Hezron and Hamul. [13]Issachar's sons: Tolah, Puvah, Iob, and Shimron. [14]Zebulun's sons: Sered, Elon, and Jahleel. [15]These are the sons of Leah, whom she bore Jacob in Paddan-aram, and his daughter Dinah. Counting every person, his sons and his daugh-

ters came to thirty-three. [16]Gad's sons: Ziphion, Haggi, Shuni, Ezbon, Eri, Arodi, and Areli. [17]Asher's sons: Imnah, Ishvah, Ishvi, and Beriah, their sister being Serah. Beriah's sons: Heber and Malchiel. [18]These are the sons of Zilpah, whom Laban gave to his daughter Leah. She bore these for Jacob, sixteen persons. [19]The sons of Jacob's wife Rachel were Joseph and Benjamin. [20]To Joseph were born in the country of Egypt Manasseh and Ephraim, whom Asenath the daughter of Potiphera, the priest of Heliopolis, bore him. [21]Benjamin's sons: Bela, Becher, Ashbel, Gera, Naaman, Ehi, Rosh, Muppim, Huppim, and Ard. [22]These are the sons of Rachel who were born to Jacob, counting every person fourteen. [23]Dan's son: Hushim. [24]Naphtali's sons: Jahzeel, Guni, Jezer, and Shillem. [25]These are the sons of Bilhah, whom Laban gave to his daughter Rachel. She bore these for Jacob, counting every person, seven. [26]Counting every person belonging to Jacob who came to Egypt, the people who came forth from his body, apart from the wives of Jacob's sons, counting every person, were sixty-six, [27]while Joseph's sons who were born to him in Egypt were two. Counting every person belonging to Jacob's household who came down to Egypt, seventy.

[28]Judah was the one he sent ahead of him to Joseph to show the way before him to Goshen. So they came to the region of Goshen, [29]and Joseph harnessed his chariot and came up to meet his father Israel in Goshen. When he appeared before him, he threw his arms round his neck and wept on his neck again and again. [30]Israel said to Joseph, "I can die now, after I have seen your face, seen that you are still alive." [31]Joseph said to his brothers and his father's household, "I will go up and tell Pharaoh, and say to him, "My brothers and my father's household, who were in the country of Canaan—they have come to me. [32]The men are shepherds, because they have been livestock men, and their flocks and their cattle and all that is theirs—they have brought it. [33]So when Pharaoh summons you and says, 'What is your work,' [34]say, 'Your servants have been livestock men from our youth until now, both we and our ancestors,' so that you may live in the region of Goshen, because all shepherds are an offense to Egyptians."

Introducing Genesis 44 I referred to one incident in the life of a man and a woman; then, introducing Genesis 45, I referred to an aspect of my wife's and my life. In different ways, both stories show how at the time something happens, you can never see the entire significance of a particular incident. There is an ancient Greek saying that urges people to call no one happy until they are dead. It is not the gloomy statement it at first sounds; it means that only at the end of someone's life is it possible to make a judgment, when you can look at the life as a whole.

The stories of Abraham and Isaac comprise a collection of separate accounts of individual events in their lives. There are few links between them, though you do get some extra insight into the significance of each individual story when you read it as part of a whole; but you can read each of the stories on its own and get quite a lot of its point. That's not so with the Joseph story (the Jacob story is somewhere in between). In this book, the ratio of text to my comment in considering the Joseph story is different from what it was through most of the rest of Genesis. It is not because I have run out of space or energy but because it is a different kind of story. The episodes are all interconnected, and when you read one chapter on its own, it has much less significance in isolation from the rest than is the case earlier in Genesis. There is a theological point here. The earlier stories show God involved in the individual incidents in someone's life. The Joseph story shows God involved in the long haul of a life. It shows how experiences and events are interconnected, with God involved in the interconnections.

This present chapter reminds us of a related point. I have referred to it as the Joseph story, but actually it is the Jacob story. It began by telling us this in Genesis 37:1. The story relates how Jacob and his family ended up in Egypt. So not only do the individual episodes in Joseph's story need to be seen in the context of the drama of his life as a whole but the Joseph drama as a whole also needs to be seen in that wider context. In the West we are often especially interested in what happens to individuals; we focus on our own importance as individuals. Genesis reckons that the broader drama of God's purpose is also important. Joseph's story is part of Jacob's story, and Jacob's story is part of the story of God's fulfilling a purpose for the world as a whole. One reason it may also be our story is that it may illustrate dynamics present in our lives. But it is definitely our story for another reason: we are the heirs of what God did back then. As Christians we enjoy God's blessing because God set going an intention to bless the world by means of Abraham and Sarah and their family, and the Joseph story is part of that. We are indebted to Joseph.

So Jacob goes down to Egypt. It is the means whereby the family will not only survive but flourish and whereby that purpose of God's will not only stay on track but advance. In light of the way the story will unfold in Exodus, there is some irony in this fact. For Israelites listening to the story, Egypt was chiefly a place of oppression and bondage, yet it starts off as a place of refuge, rescue, and growth. One would be hesitant to go down to Egypt, and it would not be surprising if Jacob himself is hesitant about leaving **Canaan**. When he was on his way out of Canaan on the run from Esau, God appeared to him at Bethel (Genesis 28). Now he is on his way out in the opposite direction. The country can be described as extending from Dan in the north to Beersheba in the south, for practical purposes Beersheba marks its southern boundary, since between Beersheba and Egypt there is only desert. At the beginning of this chapter it is as if Jacob hesitates for a moment at Beersheba. So there God appears to him again, once more telling him that things will be OK. God will be with him in going and with him in coming back (for his burial in the land of promise).

The Egyptians' aversion for shepherds is perhaps an aspect of their aversion to foreigners (Genesis 43:28 referred to their dislike of eating with foreigners). As shepherds, Jacob's family were not a settled people, and unsettled peoples often make settled people feel uneasy. Like other immigrant communities, the family members therefore end up living together rather than living among their host community, but that may facilitate their staying together and not losing their identity.

GENESIS 47:1–26

Nationalization

¹Joseph came and told Pharaoh, "My father and my brothers, and their flocks and their cattle and all that is theirs—they have come from the country of Canaan. Yes, they are in the region of

Goshen." [2]He took some of his brothers, five of them, and presented them before Pharaoh. [3]Pharaoh said to his brothers, "What is your work?" They said to Pharaoh, "Your servants are shepherds, both we and our ancestors." [4]They said to Pharaoh, "It is to stay in the country as migrants that we have come, because there is no pasture for your servants' flocks because the famine is severe in the country of Canaan, so that now your servants may please live in the region of Goshen." [5]Pharaoh said to Joseph, "Given that your father and your brothers have come to you, [6]the country of Egypt is before you. Have your father and your brothers live in the best part of the country, in the region of Goshen, and if you know that there are some capable men among them, make them livestock-heads over all that is mine."

[7]Joseph brought his father Jacob and presented him before Pharaoh, and Jacob blessed Pharaoh. [8]Pharaoh said to Jacob, "How many are the years of your life?" [9]Jacob said to Pharaoh, "The years of my stay are one hundred and thirty. Few and hard have been the years of my life; they have not reached the years of the lives of my ancestors during their stay." [10]So Jacob blessed Pharaoh and left Pharaoh's presence, [11]and Joseph settled his father and his brothers and gave them a holding in the country of Egypt, in the best part of the country, in the region of Rameses, as Pharaoh had instructed. [12]Joseph provided for his father and his brothers and all his father's household with food according to the number of the little ones.

[13]But food: there was none in the country, because the famine was very severe. The country of Egypt and the country of Canaan withered because of the famine. [14]Joseph collected all the money that was to be found in the country of Egypt and in the country of Canaan in payment for the grain that they were buying. Joseph brought the money to Pharaoh's house. [15]When the money from the country of Egypt and the country of Canaan came to an end, all Egypt came to Joseph saying, "Give us food: why should we die in front of you? Because money is gone." [16]Joseph said, "Bring your livestock, and I will give it to you in exchange for your livestock, if money is gone." [17]So they brought their livestock to Joseph and Joseph gave them food in exchange for the horses, for the stocks of sheep, for the stocks of cattle, and for the donkeys. He provided them with food in exchange for all their livestock that year. [18]When that year came

to an end, they came to him the next year and said to him, "We will not hide from my lord that the money has come to an end, and the animal stocks belong to my lord: there is nothing left before my lord except our bodies and our land. [19]Why should we die before your eyes, both we and our land? Take possession of us and our land in exchange for food. We ourselves and our land will be serfs to Pharaoh. Give seed, so that we may live and not die, and our land not become a waste."

[20]So Joseph took possession of all the land in Egypt for Pharaoh, because the Egyptians, each of them, sold their fields because the famine was so tough for them, and the country came to belong to Pharaoh. [21]And the people: he caused them to move into the cities from one end of Egypt to the other. [22]However, he did not take possession of the priests' land, because the priests had a statutory allotment from Pharaoh and they ate their allotment that Pharaoh gave them. Thus they did not sell their land. [23]Joseph said to the people, "Now. Today I have taken possession of you and your land for Pharaoh. Here is seed for you. You will sow the land, [24]and at the harvests you will give a fifth to Pharaoh, and four-fifths will be yours, as seed for the fields and as food for you and for those in your households, and as food for your little ones." [25]They said, "You have kept us alive. We have found favor in the eyes of my lord. We will be serfs to Pharaoh." [26]Joseph made it a statute until this day for the land in Egypt: a fifth is Pharaoh's. However, the priests' land alone did not become Pharaoh's.

In the recession of 2008 and its aftermath, a new *n*-word was uttered in hushed tones in the United States. To many people, "nationalization" was as frightening a notion as government-organized health insurance. But the question had to be asked: Was this the best way, or even the only way, to deal with the perilous state of banks and auto companies? Whereas European countries were willing enough to act on this assumption, it is not the U.S. way.

Joseph is the Bible's great nationalizer. He exercises power in Egypt at a moment of great crisis, a crisis he knew was coming and one with which he knows how to cope. There is little hint in the story of any awareness that there might be another way to cope with it or any awareness that there might be a downside to his action. One might think the backstory is jaw-droppingly similar to ones that occur in our world. Egypt and **Canaan** know years of prosperity (part of the background is that for long periods Canaan, while nominally a country of independent city-states, was part of a broader mini-empire under Egyptian control). Through that period they live well, but no one except Joseph would have given a thought to the future. Presumably Joseph is able to store the surplus grain of the good years because he buys it from the people, and presumably the fact of the surplus means he doesn't have to pay much for it. One might even imagine Egyptian farmers laughing all the way to the bank at Joseph's paying them for grain no one is ever going to need. Whereas they could have stored it up for themselves, selling it and/or eating well and/or using the money to build swimming pools in their yards seems a better idea. . . . Then, when they need to buy it back from Joseph, it will not be surprising if they find the price has gone up.

Maybe there is no way out of that dynamic, as perhaps there is no way of avoiding recessions. They are caused by human weakness and greed. And maybe there is no way out of their losing their lands and their freedom as a result. But it feels as if there is something wrong with a process whereby everybody ends up as Pharaoh's servants or serfs or slaves. Hebrew uses the same word for all three of these meanings. The people were not slaves in the sense that the United States has known slavery but were more like sharecroppers who previously had their own land, freedom, and independence. The reference to moving them into cities is surprising, and modern translations assume the text has been changed, but the reference recalls the way developments like this result in a flight to the cities and to peasants' having to commute from there to farm the land that was once their own but has come into the control of big landowners.

The deepest irony is that the serfdom Joseph introduces naturally embraces his own family and dependents. It means that eventually they will need to be rescued from "the household of serfs." By then they are evidently in a more subservient position than other people, because such is often the fate of a foreign community present in a country on sufferance, especially when the economy goes south. Perhaps it would have happened without Joseph's action, or perhaps it is a typical example of the way governments and other bodies have to make decisions that seem the best ones at the time but that have consequences they cannot foresee and that make us wish (with 20-20 hindsight) they had acted differently.

In another context, Jacob's blessing Pharaoh might imply no more than his greeting Pharaoh, but the fact that Genesis twice tells us about this blessing confirms that in this context it takes up a key theme. Remember, Joseph's story is part of his father's story, and thus of his grandfather's and great-grandfather's story, which begins with God's promise that he and his descendants are to be a means of blessing to the nations. Joseph has been bringing that about, in an admittedly equivocal way. Jacob's blessing Pharaoh is a sacramental sign of it.

GENESIS 47:27–48:22

The Younger Again Ahead of the Elder

[27]The Israelites lived in the country of Egypt in the region of Goshen. They acquired holdings in it, they were fruitful, and they became very numerous. [28]Jacob lived seventeen years in the country of Egypt, and Jacob reached a hundred and forty-seven years of age. [29]When the time drew near for Israel to die, he called his son Joseph and said to him, "If I have found favor in your eyes, will you put your hand under my thigh and act in commitment and steadfastness to me: please do not bury me in Egypt. [30]When I lie down with my ancestors, transport me from Egypt and bury me in their burial place." He said, "I will act in accordance with your word." [31]He said, "Swear to me." So he swore to him. Israel bowed low at the head of the bed.

[48:1]After these things happened, it was told Joseph, "Now. Your father is ill." He took his two sons with him, Manasseh and Ephraim. [2]Jacob was told, "Here, your son Joseph has come to you." Israel summoned his strength and sat up on the bed. [3]Jacob said to Joseph, "El Shadday, he appeared to me at Luz in the country of Canaan and blessed me, [4]and said to me, 'So then I am making you fruitful and numerous and making you a community of peoples and giving this country to your offspring after you as an agelong holding." [5]And now, your two sons who were born to you in the country of Egypt before my coming to you in Egypt: they are mine. [6]Your progeny who are born to you after them will be yours. In the name of their brothers they will be recorded in their inheritance. [7]While I myself was coming from Paddan, alas Rachel died, in the country of Canaan, on the journey, when I was still a distance from reaching Ephrath, and I buried her there on the road to Ephrath" (that is, Bethlehem).

[8]So when Israel saw Joseph's sons, he said, "Who are these?" [9]Joseph said to his father, "They are my sons, whom God has given me here." He said, "Will you bring them to me so that I may bless them?" [10]Now Israel's eyes were dim because of age. He could not see. He brought them near to him, and he kissed them and hugged them. [11]Israel said to Joseph, "To see your face! I did not expect it. And here—God has let me see your offspring as well." [12]Joseph removed them from his knees and bowed low, with his face to the ground. [13]Joseph took the two of them, Ephraim with his right hand, to Israel's left, and Manasseh with his left hand, to Israel's right, and brought them near to him. [14]Israel put out his right hand and put it on Ephraim's head (though he was the younger) and his left hand on Manasseh's head, crossing his hands, because Manasseh was the firstborn, [15]and he blessed Joseph, saying, "May the God before whom my fathers Abraham and Isaac walked, the God who has been shepherding me from whenever until this day, [16]the aide who has restored me from all trouble, bless the boys. Through them may my name be recalled, and the names of my fathers Abraham and Isaac. May they teem numerously in the midst of the earth." [17]Joseph saw that his father was going to put his right hand on Ephraim's head and it seemed wrong to him, and he took his father's hand so as to move it from Ephraim's head to Manasseh's head. [18]Joseph said to his father, "Not like that, father, because this one is the firstborn. Place your right hand on his head." [19]But his father refused and said, "I know, son, I know. He will become a people as well, he will become great as well, but nevertheless his younger brother will be greater than him, and his offspring will become a full number of nations." [20]So that day he blessed them: "By you Israel will bless, saying, 'God make you like Ephraim and Manasseh.'" And he put Ephraim before Manasseh.

[21]Israel said to Joseph: "Now. I am going to die, but God will be with you and will take you back to the country of your

fathers. [22]And to you I give one shoulder above your brothers, which I took from the control of the Amorites with my sword and my bow."

I have known more than one grandfather who made a nuisance of himself by whipping out a folder of photographs of his grandchildren at the slightest provocation, to inflict them on other people. I understand the intensity of one's feeling about one's grandchildren even though I don't express it like that. I have a vivid memory of my son calling late one Sunday night to tell me that our first grandchild had been born on Monday (the time difference between the United States and Britain can be confusing). I rushed to buy a plane ticket, and I have a vivid memory of taking the baby for walk in his stroller as I had taken his father for such walks. That older memory was so vivid that it seemed to have happened yesterday. So was I John and was this my son, or was I my son, and is this his son? It provoked another memory. When my wife and I married, it was really our parents' special occasion, and our children belonged to them, too (a generation later, our being six thousand miles away at least protected our son and daughter-in-law from that).

Jacob is also a bit confused, partly for comparable reasons. Joseph was almost his youngest son, but he was his "first" son because he was the son of the great love of his life, the son for whom he and Rachel had waited as Abraham and Sarah had waited and Isaac and Rebekah had waited. He is also the son who means all the more to him because of his beloved's untimely death in giving birth to her other son Benjamin. So as grandfather, Jacob claims Joseph's sons as his own. There are other reasons that he does so. One is that they were born in Egypt (and have an Egyptian mother), and it might seem questionable whether they have a right to inherit the family promise in **Canaan**. Jacob makes sure they count as his family. That concern links with a motif running through the last chapters of Genesis. It cannot be that this family is settling in Egypt forever. Jacob knows it is not the land of promise. He wants to be buried in Canaan with his family, not in this foreign country, and he gets Joseph to swear a solemn oath in this connection,

171

like the one Abraham had once had his servant swear (see the comment on Genesis 24). His bowing low on his bed is perhaps an expression of his gratitude and relief, but it is also another fulfillment of Joseph's dream.

We can see further significance in his action when we look back once more from the perspective of the people listening to the story. Levi's descendants will become the priestly clan, leaving the people as a whole with only eleven "regular" clans, so the two groups that trace their ancestry to Joseph become two clans in order to make up the number twelve. Further, the odd fact that **Ephraim** is the more powerful of the two illustrates a recurring feature of the Genesis story. It is not surprising that Jacob should put the younger ahead of the elder because as Isaac's younger son he had maneuvered his way ahead of the elder brother. And God was once again willing to go along because it resisted the conventions of power and importance that society affirms.

There is another odd fact that illustrates that same principle. Together, Ephraim and Manasseh will be the dominant clans in the northern part of the country, even though the ancestors after whom they are named are not Jacob's own sons. Joseph is almost Jacob's youngest son, and his brothers know it and he knows it, yet God turns his descendants into the largest clans, notwithstanding the possibility that he is really rather a bumptious lad. This rise to a position of dominance is suggested by Jacob's reference to giving Joseph a "shoulder" above his brothers. The word may here suggest a "ridge," though we don't know anything else about Jacob's closing reference to his taking control of the area from its former inhabitants. More significantly, the word is *shechem*, the name of a key city in Ephraim that has been important in the Genesis story. Jacob's words are another veiled allusion to the way Joseph's descendants will come to be so important in the centuries to come.

Many of the paragraphs in this part of the story are jumpy or repetitive; the third paragraph in this chapter's Scripture selection seems to take us behind the second, or give us an overlapping version of the story. In addition, the story moves between using the name "Jacob" and "Israel." This may again reflect the way Genesis has combined different existing versions of the same story—for instance, one that used the name "Jacob" and one that used his new name "Israel." Genesis didn't want to abandon any of the material in different versions of the story, so it included both.

GENESIS 49:1–28

Deathbed Promises and Predictions

[1]Jacob called his sons and said, "Gather together and I will tell you what is to befall you in days to come. [2]Assemble and listen, sons of Jacob, listen to your father Israel.

> [3]Reuben, you are my firstborn, my strength and the firstborn of my vigor, excelling in rank and excelling in power. [4]Turbulent as water, you will not excel, because you climbed into your father's bed, then you defiled it; he climbed my couch.
> [5]Simeon and Levi are brothers; their pikes are violent weapons. [6]May my person not come into their council, may my soul not join in their assembly; because when they were angry they slew someone, as they pleased they hamstrung an ox. [7]Cursed be their anger because it is fierce, their outburst because it is ferocious. I will divide them in Jacob, scatter them in Israel.
> [8]You are Judah; your brothers will 'confess' you. With your hand on your enemies' neck, your father's sons will bow down to you. [9]Judah is a lion cub; from prey, son, you have come up. You have bent down, lain like a lion, like a lioness—who will rouse him? [10]The staff will not leave from Judah, the scepter from between his feet, until tribute comes to him and the submission of the peoples is his. [11]He is one who ties his donkey to a vine, his donkey's offspring to a choice vine. He washes his clothes in wine, his garments in grape-blood. [12]His eyes are dark from wine, his teeth white from milk.
> [13]Zebulun is to dwell toward the sea shore and is to be toward the shore for ships; his flank will be at Sidon.
> [14]Issachar is a sturdy donkey lying among the sheepfolds. [15]He saw a resting place—how good it was, and the country—how beautiful. He bent his shoulder to the burden, became a conscript servant.

173

> [16] Dan is to 'govern' his people as one of the clans of Israel. [17] Dan is to be a snake by the road, a viper by the path, one that bites the horse's heels so that its rider falls backwards. [18] For your deliverance I have waited, Yahweh.
> [19] Gad: 'raiders' will 'attack' him, but he himself will 'attack' their heel.
> [20] From Asher: his food will be rich, and he will give a king's delicacies.
> [21] Naphtali is a hind set free, who gives lovely fawns.
> [22] Joseph is a fruitful branch, a fruitful branch by a spring, branches that run over a wall. [23] Archers shot at him with ferocity and assaulted him, [24] but his bow stayed firm and his arms and hands were agile, because of the hands of the Champion of Jacob, because the Shepherd, the Stone of Israel, was there, [25] because of the God of your father who helps you and Shadday who blesses you, with blessings of the heavens above, blessings of the deep lying below, blessings of the breasts and the womb. [26] Your father's blessings have been stronger than the blessings of the ancient mountains, the bounty of the age-old hills: may they come on Joseph's head, on the brow of the prince of his brothers.
> [27] Benjamin is a wolf who tears apart, in the morning he eats the prey, at evening he divides the spoil."

[28] All these are the twelve clans of Israel and this is what their father spoke to them when he blessed them, blessing each of them according to his blessing.

When you know you are going to die soon, it may concentrate the mind. You may see things more clearly. The poet Jason Shinder found his voice as a poet through the cancer that brought his death in middle age. His friends saw him as living in denial about his illness; indeed, he wrote in a short poem that he had been avoiding his illness because he was afraid he was going to die: "And when I do / I'll end up alone again," he wrote. Yet the poems he wrote during his illness brought him a kind of clarity about life. He is breathtakingly realistic about the fact that a few decades after we die, there will be no one left who knew us. Yet "the hours are left for vanishing and also for joy and for blessing and gratitude."

Jacob is the first of a line of Old Testament figures who deliver significant discourses when they are about to die. Moses, Joshua, and Samuel do the same. Jacob's is distinctive for the way it (appropriately) speaks to his sons and to their descendants, the clans bearing his sons' names. Sometimes it speaks in the future because these are events that are yet to happen; sometimes, in the present or past because they are already real in Jacob's mind's eye and in the experience of the clans. Once again we can imagine the clans listening and finding that Jacob's words answer questions they might ask.

First Jacob speaks of Leah's six sons. Reuben is the eldest brother, but his clan is a small one. Why? Reuben's attempt to bolster his position as his father's successor by sleeping with one of his father's wives (Genesis 35:22) has the opposite effect to the one he is seeking. Simeon and Levi would be next in line for leadership, so why does Simeon almost disappear and Levi get diverted into serving in the sanctuary? They disqualified themselves by their violent action against Shechem (Genesis 34). That is why **Judah**, Jacob's fourth son, found himself the ancestor of the leading clan in Israel as a whole, the one from which David and the Davidic line would come, and thus the one who will see nations submitting to his authority and see his land astonishingly fertile (abounding in wine and milk); his name links with the word for confess or give thanks (see the account of his birth in Genesis 29:35). The description of Zebulun would give the impression that the clan's land was on the coast; actually it was only *toward* the Mediterranean, in the Jezreel plain, and on the way to Phoenicia (Sidon). Issachar's land lay to the west of Zebulun with the advantage of enjoying the fertile Jezreel plain but the disadvantage of this being an area where the **Canaanites** long remained strong; Issachar's clan will be subordinate to them, but the advantages of the area will make them not mind too much.

Next are the four sons of Bilhah and Zilpah. Dan will be one of the small clans and will be forced to move from land next to Judah to a new home in the far north. Jacob's promises assure it that, as its name suggests, it will share in the rule of the clans as a whole (see Genesis 30:6): for all its apparent insignificance it does count. His prayer takes off from the pressure it will be under. Something similar applies to Gad. There are similarities between its name and words for "raid" and "attack"; it will be located in a vulnerable position east of the Jordan. In contrast, Asher will settle in an area like Issachar's that produces fine food. Napthali will enjoy the freedom of the Galilee mountains.

Finally Jacob comes to Rachel's two sons. Not surprisingly, Joseph gets most space of all, slightly more than Judah; in the future, Joseph will be the main father figure for the northern kingdom as Judah will be for the south. He will be fruitful and a survivor, as we know already from his story. But this will reflect not just his personal resources but the aid of Jacob's God, the one who grants blessing from above (rain) and below (springs), keys to the land's fruitfulness. Jacob prays that the great blessings he himself has known will come on his favorite son. Little Benjamin then gets one line that recognizes the ferocity his clan will show in the stories that follow in the Old Testament.

The importance of the blessing theme throughout Genesis makes it appropriate that this should be prominent as the book draws to an end, and the motif's importance to Jacob makes it an appropriate one for Jacob himself to emphasize. At the same time, the importance of "fairness" in Western thinking may make Jacob's differentiated blessings troubling to us, as it has raised questions at other points in Genesis. Why aren't all the brothers given equal (even if different) blessings? I don't know the answer to that, but I do know that Jacob's blessings correspond to the way human life always works. Different people have more brain power or more physical skills, or live in more favorable climates or more peaceful times. For the brothers and for us, the question is what we do with what we have.

GENESIS 49:29–50:26

Am I in the Place of God?

²⁹He instructed them and said to them, "I am going to join my kin. Bury me with my fathers in the cave that is in the field of Ephron the Hittite, ³⁰the cave that is in the field at Machpelah which is east of Mamre, in the country of Canaan, the field that Abraham acquired from Ephron the Hittite as a burial holding

³¹(there they buried Abraham and his wife Sarah, there they buried Isaac and his wife Rebekah, there I buried Leah), ³²the field and the cave that is in it acquired from the Hittites." ³³Jacob finished instructing his sons and drew his feet into the bed, breathed his last and joined his kin. ⁵⁰:¹Joseph fell on his father's face and kissed him.

²Joseph instructed the physicians who were his servants to embalm his father. When the physicians embalmed Israel, ³they took forty days for him, because that is how they complete the days for embalming. The Egyptians wept for him seventy days, ⁴and when the days of weeping for him had passed, Joseph spoke to Pharaoh's household: "If I find favor in your eyes, will you speak in Pharaoh's ears and say, 'My father himself got me to swear, "Now. I am going to die. In the tomb that I dug for myself in the country of Canaan, there you are to bury me." So may I now go up and bury my father, and come back?'" ⁶Pharaoh said, "Go up and bury your father as he got you to swear."

⁷So Joseph went up to bury his father. All Pharaoh's servants went up with him, and the senior people in his household, all the senior people in the country of Egypt, ⁸all Joseph's household, his brothers, and his father's household. Only the little ones, and their flocks and their cattle, did they leave in the region of Goshen. ⁹Both chariots and horsemen went up with him. It was a very large company. ¹⁰They came to the threshing floor at Atad, which is beyond the Jordan, and held a very great and solemn lamentation there. He observed seven days of mourning for his father. ¹¹The Canaanite inhabitants of the country saw the mourning at the threshing floor at Atad and said, "This is a serious mourning on the part of the Egyptians." Hence it was called "The Mourning of the Egyptians," which is beyond the Jordan.

¹²So his sons did for him as he had instructed them. ¹³His sons transported him to the country of Canaan and buried him in the cave in the field at Machpelah, the field that Abraham acquired as a burial holding from Ephron the Hittite, east of Mamre. ¹⁴Joseph went back to Egypt, he and his brothers and all the people who had gone up with them to bury his father, after they had buried his father.

¹⁵When Joseph's brothers saw that their father was dead, they said, "What if Joseph feels hostile to us and really gets back at us for all the wrong that we did to him?" ¹⁶So they gave instructions

to Joseph: "Your father gave instructions before his death: [17]'Say this to Joseph, "Will you forgive your brothers' affront and their offenses, because they did wrong to you?"' So will you now forgive the affront of the servants of your father's God?" Joseph wept when they spoke to him. [18]His brothers also came and fell before him and said, "Here are we as servants to you." [19]Joseph said to them, "Don't be afraid. Am I in the place of God? [20]Whereas you yourselves intended wrong for me, God intended it for good, so as to act today to keep alive a numerous people. [21]So now, don't be afraid. I myself will provide for you and your little ones." Thus he comforted them and encouraged them.

[22]So Joseph lived in Egypt, he and his father's household. Joseph lived a hundred and ten years [23]and saw the third generation of Ephraim; the children of Machir, son of Manasseh, were also born on Joseph's knees. [24]Then Joseph said to his brothers, "I am going to die, but God will definitely deal with you and take you up from this country that he swore to Abraham, to Isaac, and to Jacob." [25]Joseph got the Israelites to swear, "God will definitely deal with you, and you are to take up my bones from here." [26]So Joseph died at the age of a hundred and ten. They embalmed him and he was put in a coffin in Egypt.

A year or two ago, the Roman Catholic Archbishop of Los Angeles, Cardinal Roger Mahoney, was attacked one night near the cathedral. According to reports that surfaced somewhat later, he was punched, knocked to the ground, and kicked. But these reports did not emerge at the time because he did not report the assault but later spoke of it in an address to the priests in his diocese, which was how the news got into the press and onto TV.

When you have been wronged, you want justice. Cardinal Mahoney, who was in his seventies at the time, might not have been able to get back at his assailant. One might have expected him to report the attack to the police, but he knew the likely background to the man's attack, an indignation at sexual abuse by priests, and thus did nothing.

Joseph's brothers knew it would be natural for Joseph to want justice, though the plan they hatch to avoid his taking justice is laughably pathetic. Joseph does not even point out how patent are their lies. It is as well for his brothers that he has this totally other framework for looking at events. I don't know that Cardinal Mahoney articulated the awareness that he was not in God's place, that getting justice was not his business, but it would be an implication of his inaction. He "carried" the man's wrongdoing; that is the literal meaning of the word for "forgive," the word Abraham uses in Genesis 18 in urging God to "carry" Sodom's wrongdoing. When we forgive someone, we take responsibility for the effect of their wrongdoing and its consequences, even though the responsibility really belongs to them. We refuse to let it have the effect that it logically should have. There is not much indication that the brothers feel contrite about the wrong they did. Their dominant feeling is simply fear for their own future. What if Joseph relates to them in the way they related to him? But notwithstanding the way he may have been trying to drive them to repentance earlier, Joseph does not ask himself questions about whether contrition is a necessary condition for forgiveness. He knows he must carry their wrongdoing, as he has been doing for most of his life. If there is some ambiguity about the way he treated them earlier, there is none here.

It is as well for the brothers that there is this other element in Joseph's framework for looking at events: they intended wrong for him, but God intended it for good so as to keep the family alive. Joseph restates the point he made in chapter 45. He does not imply God planned for the brothers to do what they did. Maybe God did, but he does not say that, and it would be an odd thing for God to do (God would surely be able to plan something that involved less suffering). What the story more likely illustrates is that God can take a negative human intention and turn it into something that can have a positive effect. When people talk about God's doing that in their lives, they often refer to God's bringing good in a person's life out of a wrong done to one person or out of something regrettable that happens. Joseph's point is a bolder one. Through something wrong done to him God did something good for other people. The supreme example is the story of the wrong done to Jesus. In Joseph's story and Jesus' story, at least, it is on the large scale, in events that have universal implications, that God coolly takes the most wicked of human acts and turns them into acts that can achieve something. It does not happen all the time, but God can make it happen.

So Genesis comes to an end. As I noted in the introduction to this book, its end is a little like the end of series one of a drama on TV. Genesis comes to a semicolon (and a question mark) not a full stop or period. The stress on Jacob's blessing in these chapters suggests that God's promise to Abraham and his descendants has found some fulfillment. Here, the Egyptians' astonishing recognition of Jacob's importance suggests more fulfillment. The comment on Jacob's family indeed being a numerous people suggests yet more. But the note that Joseph's family is still in Egypt, as are Joseph's bones, makes clear that not all is fulfilled. Paradoxically, the stress on Jacob's burial in **Canaan** along with members of his family also emphasizes this lack of fulfillment. They all rest in the promised land; Joseph and his brothers do not.

The scriptwriter wants us to come back in the fall to find out what happens next, how the rest of God's promise finds fulfillment. Fortunately we live after the rest of the series has been shown, and we can download it straightaway (that is, we can turn over the page into Exodus).

GLOSSARY

aide

A supernatural agent through whom God may appear and work in the world. Standard English translations refer to them as "angels," but this designation is inclined to suggest ethereal figures with wings, wearing diaphanous white dresses. Aides are humanlike figures; hence it is possible to give them hospitality without realizing who they are (Hebrews 13). And they have no wings; hence their need of a stairway or ramp between heaven and earth (Genesis 28). They appear in order to act or speak on God's behalf and so fully represent God that they can speak as if they *are* God (Genesis 22). They thus bring the reality of God's presence, action, and voice without bringing such a real presence that it would electrocute mere mortals or shatter their hearing.

altar

A structure for offering a sacrifice (the word comes from the word for sacrifice), made of earth or stone. An altar might be relatively small, like a table, and the person making the offering would stand in front of it. Or it might be higher and larger, like a platform, and the person making the offering would climb onto it.

Aram, Aramaeans, Aramaic

In the period to which Genesis refers, the Aramaeans were a people living in Syria and northern Mesopotamia. Aram later became the name for a more defined political entity in Syria, **Ephraim**'s big, northeastern neighbor; English translations then often refer to it as Syria. The Aramaic language, a sister language of Hebrew somewhat in the way Spanish is a sister language of Portuguese or Italian, became the international language of the Middle East. Parts of Ezra, Jeremiah, and Daniel are in Aramaic, and it was the everyday language of Palestine in Jesus' day.

Canaan, Canaanites

"Canaan" designates the country of Israel as a whole; "Canaanites" refers to the whole country's indigenous peoples. It is thus not so much the name of a particular ethnic group as a shorthand term for all the peoples native to the country. "Amorites" can be used in a similar way.

commitment

"Commitment" is the word *hesed*, which English translations render in many different ways: steadfast love, constant love, kindness, mercy, loving-kindness, grace, favor, loyalty, or just love. It denotes what happens when someone makes a commitment to someone else in one of two circumstances. One is when there is no prior relationship between the parties, so that someone makes a commitment he or she is under no obligation to make. The other is when there is a relationship but one of the parties shows a commitment going beyond anything one might have expected. God behaves that way toward people and rejoices when they behave that way in response. But in Genesis, the focus lies on the way people show commitment to one another.

covenant

Whereas contracts and treaties assume a quasi-legal system for resolving disputes and administering justice, a system that can be invoked if someone does not keep a commitment, in a relationship that does not work within a legal framework a person who fails to keep a commitment cannot be taken to court for doing so. With such relationships, a covenant involves some formal procedure that confirms the seriousness of the solemn commitment one party makes to another. Abraham is in covenant relationship with some people living in the same area (Genesis 14). God seals a covenant with Abraham by a ritual and later requires Abraham to seal it by accepting the sign of circumcision (Genesis 15 and 17). Abraham and Abimelech make a covenant to resolve tensions in their peoples' relationship; Isaac and Abimelech do the same (Genesis 21 and 26). Laban and Jacob make a covenant to resolve tensions in their relationship (Genesis 31). Covenants can thus be one-sided or two-sided; it is the solemn commitment that is their essence.

effigies

Genesis 31 relates how Rachel stole Laban's effigies (*teraphim*), which Laban later calls his "gods." The Old Testament can use this word for "gods" (*elohim*) to refer to a wider range of beings than the word "god" suggests in English. It can denote any beings other than ordinary humans. That would include beings we might call angels or demons and also dead people insofar as they were assumed to be in some sense still existing. In Genesis 39, Laban refers to what he has discovered through "divination," and one form of divination involves trying to discover things by consulting the dead. The "gods" would be important in that connection. They would not be images of gods (in our sense) but effigies of family members who had passed (a little like family photographs) whom people would seek to consult on the assumption that they might now know things that their relatives who were still alive could not know.

El

The word *El* is used both as a noun meaning "God" or "god" and also as if it is a name parallel to names such as **Yahweh**. In this it is actually similar to the English word *God*. In **Canaanite** religion El is the name of the senior god among all the gods. It can then be compounded with another word so as to suggest a particular angle on who God is. For instance, for Melchizedek, God is El Elyon, which means High God. For Hagar, God is El Roi, "God of my seeing/looking," which could imply "The God who sees me/looks at me/looks out for me" or "the God whom I have seen/looked out for." For Abraham, God is El **Shadday.** The fact that Melchizedek the Jebusite and Hagar the Egyptian also use this sort of name for God points to this being a way of speaking of God that Israel and its ancestors can share with other peoples.

El Shadday

El Shadday (or simply Shadday) is a name for God that the Old Testament especially associates with the time when the name **Yahweh** would not have been known and with people who would not have known that name. Thus it comes in Genesis, and it is used in connection with non-Israelites such as Balaam and Job. We do not know the meaning of the name. There are similar-looking words that mean destruction, breast, and—in a sister language of Hebrew—mountain, so it could originally have meant destructive God or nourishing God or mountainlike God, but we have little evidence that people made any of those connections in the Old Testament. The Greek translation of the Old Testament often rendered it "Almighty," and this also became the convention in English translations. But the significance of the word is that it signifies that we are talking about the true God in a way that people who do not know the name Yahweh could use. See also **El**.

Ephraim

After the reign of David and Solomon, the nation of Israel split into two. Most of the twelve Israelite clans set up an independent state in the north, separate from **Judah** and Jerusalem and from the line of David. Because this was the bigger of the two states, politically it kept the name Israel, which is confusing because Israel is still the name of the people of God as a whole. In the prophets, it is sometimes difficult to tell whether "Israel" refers to the people of God or just to the northern state. But sometimes the state is referred to by the name of one of its largest clans, Ephraim, and using this term to refer to that northern state can reduce the confusion.

exile, exilic, exiled

In the eighth century the Assyrians exiled the people of **Ephraim** from their country. Then at the end of the seventh century Babylon became the major power in Judah's world, but **Judah** was inclined to rebel against its authority, and as part of a successful campaign to get Judah to submit properly to its authority, in 597 and in 587 BC the Babylonians transported many people from Jerusalem to Babylon. They made a special point of transporting people in leadership positions, such as members of the royal family and the court, priests, and prophets (Ezekiel was one of them). These people were thus compelled to live in Babylonia for the next fifty years or so. People still in Judah were also under Babylonian authority, so they were not physically in exile, but they were also living *in* the exilic period of time. In a number of books in the Old Testament we can see that one of the issues they are dealing with is the pressures this experience brings to people.

faithfulness

In English Bibles this Hebrew word (*sedaqah*) is usually translated "righteousness," but it denotes a particular slant on what we might mean by righteousness. It means doing the right thing by the people with whom one is in a relationship, the members of one's community. Thus it is really closer to "faithfulness" than "righteousness."

Hebrew

Oddly, whereas this word eventually became the term for the language of the Jewish people and Hebrews came to be a term for the Jewish people themselves, "Hebrew" seems not to be an ethnic term in the Old Testament. While the **Israelites** might be termed Hebrews, they were not the only Hebrews, and Abraham can be designated a Hebrew (Genesis 14:13). Other languages have related words, and all seem to be more sociological than ethnic terms, a little like "gypsy." They suggest people who do not belong to a regular, recognized political community.

Israel, Israelites

Originally, Israel was the new name God gave Abraham's grandson, Jacob. His twelve sons were then forefathers of the twelve clans that comprise the people Israel. In the time of Saul and David these twelve clans became more of a political entity, so that Israel was both the people of God and a nation or state like other nations or states. After Solomon's day, this state split into two separate states, **Ephraim** and **Judah**. Because Ephraim was by far the larger, it often continued to be referred to as Israel. So if one is thinking of the people of God, Judah is part of Israel. If one is thinking politically, Judah is not part of Israel. Once Ephraim has gone out of existence, then for practical purposes Judah *is* Israel as the people of God.

Judah, Judeans

Judah was one of the twelve sons of Jacob, then the clan that traces its ancestry to him, then the dominant clan in the southern of the two states after the time of Solomon. As a Persian province or colony, it was known as Yehud.

peace

The word *shalom* can suggest peace after there has been conflict, but it often points to a richer notion: that of fullness of life. The KJV sometimes translates it "welfare," and modern translations use words such as "well-being" or "prosperity." It suggests that everything is going well for you.

Shadday, *see* **El Shadday**

Torah

The Hebrew word for the first five books of the Bible. They are often referred to as the "Law," but this label gives a misleading impression. Genesis itself is nothing like "law," and even Exodus to Deuteronomy are not "legalistic" books. The word *torah* itself means "teaching," which gives a more correct impression of the nature of *the* Torah.

Yahweh

In most English Bibles, the word "LORD" often comes in all capitals like that, as does also sometimes the word "GOD" in similar format. These actually represent the name of God, Yahweh. In later Old Testament times, **Israelites** stopped using the name Yahweh and started to refer to Yahweh as "the Lord." The strange foreign-sounding name could give the impression that Yahweh was just **Israel**'s tribal god, and they may have wanted other people to recognize that Yahweh was the one true God; a term such as "the Lord" was one anyone could recognize. In addition, people became concerned about the warning in the Ten Commandments concerning misuse of Yahweh's name. Translations into other languages then followed suit and substituted their equivalent terms for "the Lord" in place of the name Yahweh. There are several downsides. This obscures the way God wanted to be known by name, that often the text refers to Yahweh as opposed to some other (so-called) god or lord, and that "the Lord" gives the impression that God is much more "lordly" and patriarchal than actually God is. (The form "Jehovah" is not a real word but a mixture of the consonants of Yahweh and the vowels of the word for "Lord," which were added to remind people in reading Scripture that they should say "the Lord" and not the actual name.)